Praise for *240 Beats Per Minute*

"This absorbing, ambitious blend of memoir, science, and friendship, traces in two voices the journey of Bernard Witholt, an
eminent Dutch biologist with a diseased heart and his lifelong
friend, cardiologist Roger Mills. Witholt grapples—sometimes
unconventionally—with years of tachycardia while stubbornly
attempting to sustain a vigorous life. One cannot reflect on
this compelling account without saying that it has heart in
more ways than one. Witholt brings a scientist's curiosity into
how the heart works to his problems, while Mills' interspersed,
accessible reflections on his friend's journal entries are fascinating, compassionate, and clear. This book is a gift to health
care professionals treating heart patients, to patients facing their
own conditions, and to readers open to a story about resilience
in the face of challenge, about the mechanisms of an "unruly"
heart, about the power of friendship even after death, and about
the dignity of a life well-lived."

—JAN WORTH-NELSON, Editor, *East Village Magazine*, poet,
author, and lecturer emerita, University of Michigan, Flint

"Kudos to Drs. Witholt and Mills for bringing to light one of the most important issues in contemporary medicine: the psychological impact of sophisticated medical treatments. This book is a must-read for those of us who practice high tech medicine and for our patients who spend their (remaining) lives on the cutting edge."

—PETER KOWEY, MD, FACC, FAHA, FHRS, Emeritus Chair, Cardiology, Lankenau Heart Institute, William Wikoff Smith Chair, Cardiovascular Research, Lankenau Institute of Medical Research, Professor of Medicine and Pharmacology, Jefferson Medical College

Life with an **Unruly Heart**

240 Beats
PER MINUTE

BERNARD WITHOLT, PhD

with ROGER M. MILLS, MD

RIVER GROVE
BOOKS

Published by River Grove Books
Austin, TX
www.rivergrovebooks.com

Distributed by River Grove Books

Design and composition by Greenleaf Book Group
Cover design by Greenleaf Book Group
Cover images ©iStockphoto.com/simonkr

Publisher's Cataloging-in-Publication data is available.

Print ISBN: 978-1-63299-186-7

eBook ISBN: 978-1-63299-187-4

First Edition

Contents

A Note from the Editor

In 1999, my close friend, the Dutch scientist Bernie Witholt, received a device, an implantable cardioverter defibrillator (ICD), to control ventricular tachycardia, a potentially fatal heart rhythm problem. I had completed my formal training as a cardiologist at Harvard's Peter Bent Brigham Hospital in 1975 and had spent three decades working with seriously ill patients. As I watched Bernie living with his ICD, I realized that no one really understood how patients adjusted to these devices. Cardiologists implanted the devices and said, "There, that's fixed. Next."

Bernie quickly realized that his problem was not "fixed." With his ICD, he had just traded one very serious problem for a new one (also serious but less likely to be fatal).

Today, almost twenty years later, there's growing medical literature on the quality of life for patients with implanted cardiac devices. A consensus has emerged that depression and anxiety are common problems in patients who've received an ICD. Nonetheless, this literature inevitably reflects a medical viewpoint, not the patients'. Bernie was a scientist and teacher; he wanted to share his thoughts about his heart and his ICD with others. He wrote extensively over several years, with every intention of putting his thoughts together into a book. He did not have the opportunity to do that, but his wife has allowed me to edit and arrange what he wrote.

Bernie had a PhD in biology and achieved great success in research and teaching, but when he wrote about circulatory physiology (how the heart works) and, most notably, his speculations on his arrhythmia's origin and regulation of body temperature, his ideas did not always follow currently accepted medical understanding. I have made some corrections to his notes, but they are minimal. First, because he was very smart and doctors are not always right, and second, because the critical purpose of this book is to recount how one particular patient dealt with his illness over fifteen years. This is not a physiology text.

I attempted to structure Bernie's book as a continuation of a conversation that we carried on over decades. That conversation began at Amherst College, so some background about the college in the 1960s is important. I have also added some technical information and, from time to time, made comments when, based on my thirty years of clinical practice, some particular understanding of the doctor–patient relationship is important.

To make it clear whether you are reading Bernie's words or mine, his material will appear in regular font and *mine in italics*.

Acknowledgments

If I attempt to thank every individual who has played a part in the genesis of this book, the acknowledgments will stretch almost as long as the narrative itself. This section is, by necessity, selective.

Dr. Tom Jacobs, professor of clinical medicine at Columbia and one of Bernie's roommates at Hopkins, reviewed my arrangement of Bernie's papers.

Dr. Peter Kowey, electrophysiologist and mystery writer, read an early draft of the manuscript, offered his insight, and encouraged me to keep on working. Paul Dimond, lawyer and author, read a later draft, made critically important suggestions, and encouraged me to keep on working, as did Jan Worth-Nelson, lecturer emeritus in creative writing at UM-Flint, and Tom Sullivan, career reader and teacher of English poetry. I thank all of you for your friendship, your criticism, and your support.

My wife, Katherine, cheerfully put up with my hours in front of the computer; Posie, our Labrador, demanded her regular walks and helped to keep me fresh. For the uninterrupted time, and for the interruptions, thank you both.

Finally, I give my heartfelt thanks to Bernie's wife, Renske Heddema, for her confidence and trust in sending Bernie's writing to me, allowing me a free hand in editing his work, and encouraging me to add my comments.

Roger M. Mills MD, FACP, FACC
Dexter, Michigan

Prologue

"Strangers once, we came to dwell together . . .

Now we're bound by ties that cannot sever

All our whole life thro' . . ."*

Those lines begin the Amherst College Senior Song. In 1960, we fresh-men were strangers, each of us unsure of ourselves and the other 282 members of the class. We dwelt together in the freshman dorms, we ate together in Valentine Hall, and we attended classes together. The academic environment catalyzed the bonding process. In the early 1960s, all-male Amherst still followed the "New Curriculum" of 1947 (8 a.m. classes, Saturday morning classes, required twice weekly chapel attendance, and a required swimming test). Core courses were English 1–2, History 1–2, and Physics 1–2, with no electives except the foreign language of your choice. Very soon, we were no longer strangers. Although we may not have known each other's backstories, we knew we were all in it together.

Under the circumstances, it seems odd that I did not get to know Bernie Witholt that first year. He was part of a quiet and studious crowd. In contrast, I studied hard but was drawn to the opportunity to try new athletic and social opportunities. I had never ice-skated but joined the freshman hockey team; I had never seen a lacrosse stick but joined the freshman lacrosse squad. I also had the requisite false ID and classmates who enjoyed pizza and beer at the local bar.

---

* Amherst College Senior Song. J.S. Hamilton, 1906

At the last possible moment, the final required core curriculum class opened my eyes to modern biology. Watson and Crick, with their structure of DNA, had tied evolution, ecology, and chemistry together. This was truly, deeply exciting. In the absence of any "guidance office," I figured out a survival strategy. It was simple: Watch what the smart guys are doing and then do the same. Academically, the smart guys were headed toward medical school; on the athletic side, they were excelling at the sports they had learned in secondary school.

By the spring of sophomore year, I had focused on the very real problem of meeting the academic requirements for medical school applications and getting back to rowing, something athletic that I actually knew how to do.

. . .

Bernie was an outstanding oarsman. He tried out for the freshman crew in the spring of 1961, quickly picked up the basics, and liked it. In the spring of 1962, the Amherst varsity and JV crews traveled to Florida for spring training on the water. As sophomores, we both made the cut for that trip. We drove straight through, from Amherst, Massachusetts, to Winter Park, Florida. Shortly after we arrived, Bernie vaulted a fence to pilfer a half-dozen oranges fresh from the grove's trees. Now, fresh-picked ripe oranges look nothing like what's piled in supermarkets; they are dark orange and heavily flecked with brown. Bernie offered his teammates a share of the booty from his raid, saying happily, "This is what they looked like on the trees in Brazil!" That was the first time I experienced the full force of the Witholt smile.

We became friends. Bernie's earlier success in the freshman boat made him a strong contender for a seat in the varsity eight, and he held on to it. I had rowed spring and fall for three years in secondary school but still had to prove myself. I found a place as the junior varsity bowman, so there was no competition between us for our respective seats.

When Bernie and I weren't rowing, we found common ground in our interest in biology. Bernie was already focused. He had "discovered" bacteria; they were amazing little creatures. He realized microbiology would allow him to do all sorts of interesting experiments that would yield results in reasonably short periods of time. In contrast, I found the whole field exciting and had signed up for such disparate junior year courses as ecology and comparative anatomy.

• • •

In the fall of 1962, we returned for our junior year at Amherst. Kennedy was in the White House. We had joined fraternities. Beer was easily available. We'd met some nice young women at Smith and Mount Holyoke Colleges. We were going to be biology majors. Bernie had a seat in the varsity eight, and I would stroke the JV boat.

As time passed, we got to know each other better. I discovered that Bernie was born in Holland in 1941, just after the Germans had overrun the country. After the war, his family left for Brazil. They lived in São Paolo and, later, Rio. Between moves, Bernie spent a year in one Mennonite colony in Brazil, then another back in Holland. In 1959, the Witholts immigrated to Pennsylvania, where Bernie became a self-described "multilingual puzzle" to his high school guidance counselor. The counselor initially steered him toward agriculture—but not before seeking a favor from Amherst's dean of admissions, Eugene Wilson. On the same April 1960 day, the young Dutchman (who had never heard of Amherst) was interviewed, admitted, and awarded a full scholarship.

Bernie learned that I had gone to boarding school in Indiana with scholarship support and then won a National Merit Scholarship that got me into Amherst. Hardly a preppie, I was quite reticent about my shaky finances. As I became better connected through the gym, the athletic department administrator, Mrs. Kinney, somehow learned I needed to work for spending money. She often found faculty members who needed a leaf-raker, or a football or basketball game where she could use a ticket-taker.

There was really just one problem with the medical school plan, one huge hurdle: organic chemistry.

Because of my sophomoric muddle, I couldn't complete all of the courses required for a major and the courses required for medical school in the two years I had left on scholarship at Amherst. Then inspiration struck. Bernie's family had moved to Philadelphia. The University of Pennsylvania offered a six-credit-hour organic chemistry course in summer school. If I went to summer school at Penn, we could row over the summer.

And that was how the summer of 1963 happened. Bernie had a summer job in the labs at Rohm and Haas in Philadelphia. I took organic chemistry at Penn, managed a B for the course, and then found a walk-on position as a temporary lab assistant in Dr. Rita Wetton's research lab at Penn Medical School. At the end of August, just before I left, Dr. Wetton escorted me to the medical school's admissions office and recommended me for a spot in the next year's class.

Throughout that summer, Bernie and I rowed double sculls for the Vesper Boat Club. Dave Wilmerding, a member of the US National Team coached us. We were a good pair: about the same height, weight, and willingness to train hard. I stroked; Bernie rowed bow. We won every race we finished (a loose oarlock—my error—overturned us in the President's Cup on the Potomac, or we would have won that, too). When summer school was over, and I didn't have to study until mid-night, we'd stop for a beer after rowing before I headed to my sublet apartment and he headed home.

Often, the Vesper heavyweight eight was on the water when we practiced. We gradually got to the point where we could keep up with them for 500 meters. Importantly, we learned a lot by watching them. They brought home an Olympic gold medal from Mexico City the next year.

When we returned to Amherst in the fall, we had put in hundreds of kilometers together in the double. Over our beers, we had shared thoughts about science, training, and rowing and learned to trust each other. When the 1964 season arrived, Bernie and I were elected co-captains. We won some races, lost some, and, by the end of May 1964, our college years were over.

• • •

Just about everyone has a few special people in his or her life with whom a conversation simply continues across the years. You may not see each other for a year or two, or even five; then, when you sit down together, the talking resumes where you left off. It's as if you had just had coffee together a few days ago. That long conversation defines a true friendship—the kind of friendship I shared with Bernie, my college classmate, rowing teammate, and double sculls partner.

We kept in touch. After finishing his post-doctoral training, Bernie moved back to Holland, then later to Switzerland. The phone rang at odd hours, and then I'd hear the familiar, "Hey, Roger . . . " He would call when he came to the US to give a lecture or when he came to visit family. He stopped by to visit in person whenever possible. On one occasion, I had a research meeting in Bern and was able to make a stop in Zurich. The conversation never stopped.

We shared mutual difficulties (our divorces) and tragedy (his first wife's early and unexpected death a few years after their divorce).

Although I only heard him mention it once, Bernie worked at this book's story for more than a decade while he lived with a heart problem known as paroxysmal ventricular tachycardia. When something major happened, he made notes. Two years after he died, Renske Heddema, his wife, sent me what Bernie had written, and my long conversation with my friend resumed.

In those pages, I could hear Bernie directly and openly talking about his experience of learning to live with heart disease: first with his ICD and then, later, without it. As you will see, Bernie was a scientist. As a biologist, he knew he would die because every living organism, every one of us, does. That's a given, a universal, and unalterable truth. So, for Bernie, the scientist, the approachable problem—the one that might be solved—was obvious: How do I live? Living, not dying, was always the critical issue.

Part I

THE STORY

CHAPTER 1

"A Strange Rattling in My Chest"

In early February of 1999, a broad-shouldered man in late middle age entered a crowded auditorium in Zurich, Switzerland. He stood 6'1" and weighed 190 pounds. A scientist, he was dressed neatly but casually: a tweed sports jacket, tailored slacks, and a crisply pressed dress shirt with an open collar. The man's striking features included thick, round horn-rimmed glasses, bushy eyebrows, and a gap between his upper front teeth that showed when he smiled, which he did often.

This man's life was about to change dramatically. I'll let Bernie tell you about it . . .

• • •

I was one of some 150 people at a Zurich Stock Exchange symposium on new high-tech start-ups emanating from the Swiss Federal Institute of Technology (Eidgenössische Technische Hochschule, or ETH[1]) and other Swiss universities. I came in late and, finding no seat, stood leaning against a steel railing. I did not

---

1   Bernie worked for many years at ETH Zurich. Established in 1855 as the Federal Polytechnical School, ETH Zurich is a highly regarded research university with twenty-one Nobel Prize winners to its credit.

feel good and I wondered why a few of my students, seated only a few meters away, did not jump up to offer me a chair.

About an hour after the meeting started, after the first two or three talks, I felt a strange rattling in my chest. This was new and quite unsettling. Was this a heart attack? What else might it be? I felt weak, eager to sit down, but there were no empty seats. The next speaker had just started. I looked around; no one else seemed to hear the rattling. I leaned harder into the railing. After ten or fifteen minutes, the rattling subsided; the speaker finished his presentation, and I felt better.

With the rattle gone, there seemed to be no reason to immediately leave, and so I stayed. The meeting ended a few hours later. I had no interest in chatting with other participants, so I had some juice and left. This meant negotiating stairs from the auditorium level up to the higher street level. This was unpleasant. When I reached my car, I sat contemplating what had happened. Whatever it was, it did not seem trivial. I decided to go home this time, but if it happened again, I determined to go to the emergency room at the University of Zurich hospital.

I did not have long to wait. A few days later, Renske [my wife] and I joined a friend for dinner. The waiter brought us a nice bottle of white wine, but for some reason, I was interested only in water. Within a few minutes, what I wanted most was to lie down on the floor next to the table. I also felt a little embarrassed; I did not want to spoil the evening. At the same time, although I did not feel the rattling I had experienced during the symposium earlier that week, I sensed the time had come to head to the emergency room.

An hour later, I was lying in a bed with a heart rate monitor showing a steady 240 beats per minute (bpm) and an infusion pump set up to deliver adenosine [an intravenous drug] and perhaps other compounds through my veins to bring down my heart rate.

"Why adenosine?" I wondered.

The last time I had dealt with adenosine was around 1970, in California, at the University of California San Diego School of Medicine. I was a PhD post-doc studying the uptake of radio-active carbon-labeled adenine by bacteria called *Escherichia coli* (*E. coli* [2]). By giving the bacteria labeled adenine, *E. coli* doesn't have to make DNA precursors from scratch, *de novo*, all the way from sugars and amino compounds. This means less trouble and work for the *E. coli* bacteria. Like all organisms, it prefers the least amount of effort and fuss to achieve its goals.

Meanwhile, my wife stood next to my bed looking concerned. Our dinner-partner friend walked in and started crying softly. While I found this touching, I was also interested in the two young nurses who were debating whether to add adenosine to my intravenous drip at some number of micrograms per milliliter or milligrams per milliliter. I considered whether to inform them that the two terms were not equivalent; in fact, they differed by a factor of 1,000-fold (really quite a lot). I decided to let fate do its work instead as, in fact, I felt rather good. There was no need for further action on my part. The monitor kept showing 240 bpm; several people were running in and out of my cubicle, deciding what to do next and whom to call for further steps, and reserving a bed in the intensive care unit. They generally seemed in a hurry and quite concerned.

This may have been the first time in my post-childhood life that no one expected anything from me. Something fairly important

---

2 *E.coli* normally lives in the intestines of healthy people and animals and is widely used in microbiology research labs.

seemed to be happening, but I was not in charge. I did not need to think about options, consequences, or opportunities. This was a great relief and in many ways, a new and wonderful sensation.

An hour passed, and I found myself in the intensive care unit. The adenosine had changed nothing, and now my caregivers delivered a shock to my chest. This procedure brought my heart rate down. Afterward, my intravenous fluid drip was supplemented with magnesium chloride. This caused an uncomfortable, warming sensation within my limbs.

In the morning, a gentleman with a cart loaded with echocardiographic equipment came in. Later, I learned he was one of the cardiology unit's professors, a much-lauded specialist in the echocardiography section. After examining my chest with his instruments, he pronounced me (or more precisely, my heart) to be in fine condition. Nothing wrong. Go home. He packed up his equipment and rolled his cart away.

The young doctor in charge of the half-dozen beds of the intensive care unit, perhaps an intern, had followed the brief exchange with the echocardiography specialist. He suggested I call my wife to take me home. Then he added, "Perhaps you should also have the heart rhythm specialist take a look at you . . . I can arrange for an appointment."

"Rhythmologist? Why?" I asked. "I and my heart are fine."

"Yes . . . still . . . to determine that everything is fine . . . to be on the safe side maybe? It might be better . . . "

• • •

The episode originating at the Zurich Stock Exchange began Bernie's fifteen-year struggle with recurrent ventricular tachycardia (VT), a potentially life-threating heart rhythm disturbance (or cardiac arrhythmia). He wrote the story in bits and pieces when he had the time. Although I've arranged his notes in chronological order and introduced some structure, his story sometimes takes on a stream-of-consciousness quality, and that form can be difficult to follow. At the most gripping moments, Bernie often digressed to pursue scientific topics that caught his fancy (as he did when thinking aloud about E. coli and adenosine).

As I read these notes, I wondered, "Why did a disciplined scientist so often head off into the intellectual weeds? Why didn't he organize this material as he would have outlined and written the chapters in a textbook?"

Then I realized I had seen this before. Many of my heart patients use the technique. A mother will start talking about her shortness of breath and go on to describe her daughter's wedding. A retired executive complains of chest pain and immediately transitions to his recent Alaskan fishing trip. Early in my career, I tried to pull patients back from their rambles. As I gained experience, I learned to let them go on for a bit; it's amazing how much you discover about people when you listen. As Yogi Berra said, "You can observe a lot by watching."[3]

Bernie felt more comfortable out there in the weeds with his digressions. As he said, he felt a great relief from not being in charge of his immediate care. He also found an element of relief from his mysterious illness by turning to subjects he knew. These verbal walkabouts are often a way of saying that patients feel a loss of control over their life. Very early on, Bernie sensed his illness posed a threat to the life he enjoyed: leading his academic laboratory, traveling, and rowing vigorously.

And, in Bernie's case, he had a lot to digress about—a variety of subjects. There's the conversation about his life-threatening, but poorly

---

understood, heart disease while trying to live life on his own terms. Throughout the course of his illness, Bernie wanted to understand and control his body; he needed to make sense of what he heard from his doctors. But then, isn't this what we all want?

CHAPTER 2

Electrophysiological Testing

I did, indeed, go to see a [heart] rhythm specialist a few days later.[4] After Dr. Reto Candinas had looked at the records of my emergency visit and done a few preliminary tests, he concluded I had experienced several episodes of rapid heart rate, or tachycardia. He suggested that I should have a more complete electrophysiological examination to define the nature of the tachycardia (atrial or ventricular, congenital or nondescript) and to determine how to proceed: medication, ablation, installation of an ICD, or some combination of these.

So, some weeks after my first conversation with the electrophysiologist, I was lying in a large operating theatre. Several technicians were manning various computer screens in a windowed control room. More people in scrub suits milled about my operating table, above and around which was a large X-ray setup to display the routes various catheters would follow on their way to my heart.

As he pulled catheters out of their sterile packages, Dr. Candinas told me that he enjoyed carrying out this particular

---

4   A cardiologist who has advanced training in the management of heart rhythm disorders is an *electrophysiologist*.

procedure. He picked up a scalpel to make the necessary cut. Waiting for that groin incision, I could only recall my vasectomy some twenty years earlier and the unsuccessful reversal procedure several years later.

Soon the doctor enquired how I felt and then announced that the catheters were now in place. I had felt nothing and could only admire his skill. I thought of Oswald Avery's dictum on happiness: having "an experiment that works, and doing it all the time."[5] That lore had been part of our education in graduate school back in the late 1960s. Of course, this specialist, Dr. Candinas, enjoyed doing this procedure; it was an experiment that worked.

· · ·

Doctors who do invasive procedures and surgeons who perform specialized operations will tell you they really only do one or two procedures, but they perform them hundreds and hundreds of times. I used to play tennis with a well-known cardiac surgeon who told me, "I do the same operation every time. I hit the same tennis shots every time. I hit the same golf shot every time. That's why I'm good."

When you think about it, someone who is very good at what he or she does has achieved a consistency that yields the same outstanding result each time. Therefore, if something unusual happens, it's usually not because of operator error but because something really is out of the ordinary.

This procedural consistency is just as important in science. If the experimental method is sound and consistent, then the scientist can trust the results. Important point, Bernie—as we shall see.

---

5   In 1944, Avery was one of the geneticists who worked out that DNA is the essential genomic material.

• • •

Dr. Candinas and his catheters now controlled my heart rate, and so he used the equipment to increase it. At a rate of about 300 bpm, I once again had some of the sensations I'd experienced during the tachycardia of previous weeks. Odd feelings; they were not pleasant.

The computer technicians interpreted the data collected to determine whether an ablation made sense and, if so, where this should happen. However, testing showed no evidence of defective conducting pathways. Instead, the conclusion was that my heart might have a congenital defect of some sort.

I had heard something similar about ten years earlier at the University of Groningen in the Netherlands, when I was trying to understand why my basal heart rate, usually around 60 bpm, had risen to about 90 at rest. Stress seemed a good explanation, but after having an electrocardiogram recorded while I rode an exercise bike, that cardiologist told me everything was fine . . . except for a small defect, probably inborn. Not to worry; he would see me again in ten years.

Now, ten years later, here I was, in Switzerland, seeing another cardiologist.

I had forgotten about the earlier episode, but it came back to me. Perhaps my heart did indeed have some structural deviations or defects that were now beginning to make themselves unmistakably known.

• • •

Electrophysiological studies, although highly technical, are routine. But for patients, the loss of control that occurs when lying on a table and undergoing testing is far from routine. It's a matter of handing over one's individuality, even if just temporarily.

The electrophysiological test that Bernie had involves delivering a quick series of low-intensity electrical stimuli inside the pumping chambers of the heart. Healthy individuals may respond with a couple of extra beats before very quickly resuming their normal rhythm. In contrast, patients with "inducible" ventricular tachycardia often develop a prolonged episode of arrhythmia, as Bernie did when his heart rate rose to almost 300 bpm.

After the electrophysiological testing, the conclusion that Bernie had a serious problem became inescapable. The intensive care admission and subsequent testing had produced undeniable evidence that he was experiencing episodes of a heart rhythm disturbance called ventricular tachycardia, or VT. Even the most rational patients rebel against passively accepting the initial diagnosis of a disease. As with grief, our first reactions are often anger and denial. In Bernie's thoughts, we can see his professorial persona wrestling with patient persona.

Bernie wanted what every person in a similar situation wants: a specific diagnosis, a specific prognosis, and a specific therapy. In other words, "What's wrong with me, what's going to happen to me, and what can you do to fix me?"

Sometimes modern medicine does, in fact, offer these specifics. Much more often, however, medicine employs more conditional approaches. The medical establishment says, "If this diagnosis is correct, and if you have what we think you have, then this drug (or procedure, or device) might help."

When Bernie's initial testing took place two decades ago, electrophysiology was a newborn clinical discipline. Obscure electrical heart diseases like arrhythmogenic right ventricular cardiomyopathy and catecholaminergic polymorphic ventricular tachycardia had not yet been discovered. And despite Bernie's early years in rural Brazil, I don't know if anyone ever seriously considered testing him for late-life Chagas' disease, a tropical infection that sometimes manifests later in life as VT. At that time, genetic screening programs for susceptibility to VT did not exist. In any case, after Bernie's initial testing, he had no specific diagnosis and no prognosis. There was just more uncertainty.

The good news for today's patients is that physicians feel ethically obligated to explain their reasoning. The authoritarian days of "you must have this (drug/procedure/device)" with no questions answered have ended. (Or so we physicians like to think. Sometimes medical professionals are not as tolerant of questions as we would like to believe.)

Bernie would have some questions.

CHAPTER 3

Arrhythmia? Tachycardia?

Dr. Candinas had decided that I should take a drug: amiodarone. I would take amiodarone for six weeks, after which a second electrophysiological test would help determine whether the drug had had the desired effect.[6]

Tachycardia, amiodarone, ablation, ICD: These were strange new terms, new notions.

For the first fifty-eight years of my life, I had been a reasonably healthy and fit individual. As a researcher conducting experiments, I had occasionally been near hospitals, but I had only been hospitalized once, as a six-year-old patient with a tiny hernia.

I had bouts of eczema (clearly stress related) during my first year in college and later in my first year of graduate school. I had experienced seasickness on a few ocean voyages. In my entire life, I had been bed ridden for perhaps a week's total. I'd enjoyed jogging, biking, surfing, and rowing in changing combinations for more or less my entire adult life, and except for a marvelous post-dinner cigar now and then, I did not smoke. After I'd turned thirty-five

---

6 Available in Europe since the 1960s, amiodarone has been widely used to control rapid heart rhythms; it is given as an intravenous injection or taken orally in tablet form.

or forty, red wine accompanied dinner—one or two, seldom more than three, glasses per day. So, what was happening now?

I started reading about these new notions, and in 1999, I bought the first of a series of five or six heart rate monitors. The first was a fairly simple Polar sports watch, with a chest belt to transmit heart rate information. I continued jogging a few times per week and taking walks with my wife, some ten to fifteen kilometers in the countryside around Zurich, with ascents and descents totaling two hundred to five hundred meters per walk. Or, should I say, I tried to do these things.

Dr. Candinas had suggested I consider having an implantable cardioverter-defibrillator device, or ICD. This device would protect me by stopping tachycardia when it lasted longer than a preprogrammed time interval, usually thirty seconds or so.

I started reading about ICDs and decided it was better for me to delay the installation of such a device. The longer I waited, the better they would become.

Also, I was undertaking various exercises (walking and jogging) to learn more about the conditions that led to tachycardia, and I hoped I might learn to handle incidents of tachycardia without an ICD.

I followed my instructions for the use of amiodarone. I took the drug mornings and evenings, 200 mg each time, for three weeks, to build up a store of the stuff in my body. After three weeks, I reduced the dosage to 100 mg each morning and evening. After six weeks, I might still have tachycardia but presumably at heart rates significantly lower than the 240 bpm I had experienced in my pre-medicated state.

All very interesting, but what did this actually mean?

Four weeks passed after I started on the amiodarone, and I

began to experience nightmares and occasional episodes of diarrhea. I came to see all this differently as I lay in bed mulling over
my situation.

• • •

When I take amiodarone, I swallow a pill that contains the drug,
some binding agents, and coloring materials. The pill lands in
my stomach and starts to dissolve. The drug itself then enters the
small intestine, is taken up by the cells that line the inner surface
of the intestine, and is transported to the other side of these same
cells before being transported into capillaries and ending up in
the blood.

Blood is mostly water. It contains lots of specialized cells, many
different proteins, fats and lipids, carbohydrates, small metabolites
and salts—in short, all the supply of molecules our tissues and
their cells need, plus the many cells and molecules blood requires
to carry out its other functions (besides just being a river full of
material). When your local hospital looks at blood in the laboratory, it sees and lists perhaps a dozen different proteins or protein
groups, plus many molecules that are not proteins. This is perfectly
fine for routine purposes, though systems biologists working with
much more sensitive equipment can now identify seven or eight
hundred different proteins in blood.

Still, even though it is complex, blood is mostly water; solids
only account for about 20 percent of blood's total mass. Something similar also applies to the rest of our bodies, which typically
consist of around 70 percent water and 30 percent various solids.

But biologic compounds that are not soluble in water also
exist, and they are necessary when building a cell. Every single cell

in our bodies is bounded by membranes, which define the limits and form the interface between inside and outside the cell. Without these membranes, cells cannot form. Therefore, the molecules that form membranes cannot be water-soluble. If they were, they would dissolve in the cell's aqueous content.

There are also drugs that are water-soluble and others that are not. If we assume a drug molecule makes it to the small intestine, where the intestinal inner lining's cells take it up, and then, somehow, transport it into blood, it will either dissolve into the 80 percent of bulk water comprising blood or, if it is not water-soluble, stick to various more or less fatty surfaces. If the drug molecule sticks to a protein that is nicely water-soluble, it will piggyback everywhere blood is found, just as if it were soluble based on its own properties.

Let's come back to my project: building up an amiodarone store over three weeks. Why did I need to do that? In an effort to understand a little more, I looked up the chemical structure of the molecule. It is fairly large, about three to four times as large as a glucose (sugar) molecule. Amiodarone contains the usual carbon and hydrogen atoms, plus a couple of iodine atoms.

My first glance at the chemical structure of amiodarone suggested that it would be insoluble in water and much happier in organic solvents. We call such molecules *apolar* (as opposed to *polar* water-soluble molecules, such as glucose, which dissolve in water exceedingly well). We also have a measure of polarity or apolarity (the partition coefficient), which allows us to easily predict how a molecule will behave in a mixture of polar and apolar solvents.

This is not complicated. It's just like oil-and-vinegar salad dressing. If we add salt (polar) to the oil and vinegar mix, it will dissolve in the polar vinegar. However, it will never dissolve in the oil (apolar). If, instead, we add a bit of fatty material (say, a little bit of bacon grease) to the mix, this fat will not dissolve in the vinegar but will dissolve in the oil.

In the laboratory, we quantify these observations a little more by creating a 50:50 mix of water and oil, adding a given compound X, and determining how much X is dissolved in the oily solvent and how much is in the water. The ratio between these two amounts we call the partition coefficient, or P.

The point of all this is that, when the amiodarone finally makes it to my bloodstream, it will dissolve in the oily (apolar) environments. It will not stay in the polar (watery) environment. It prefers apolar to polar environments by a million to one. So, the reason for taking amiodarone for three weeks before reducing the dose is because it sticks to every oily surface it finds inside my body. Only when I have taken enough amiodarone to coat my available oily sites can it do what needs to be done to control my heart beat.

How much amiodarone will I take up during those first three weeks? At 400 mg per day, it amounts to a total of 8.4 g, most of which simply remains stuck on various oily surfaces and in oily material. During the following three weeks, taking only 200 mg per day, I would accumulate another 4.2 g, some of which may gradually be processed in the liver or disposed of in the kidneys. However, about 10 g remains somewhere in my body if I take this drug as prescribed.

Now, what about this amiodarone? How does this chemical fit among all those chemicals that collectively comprise you and me?

Amiodarone probably does its work by interacting with and binding to one or more proteins that are instrumental in regulating the heart rate. This could be a specific interaction, meaning that particular atoms of the amiodarone molecule interact with particular atoms of a protein molecule.

Alternatively, it could be a non-specific interaction. The drug might bind somewhere on the protein, for instance, because there are apolar amino acids in a region easily accessible to the drug. As we have seen, amiodarone prefers apolar areas rather than staying dissolved in watery environments.

Membranes and Amiodarone

The amount of amiodarone that ends up in my body, and the behavior and effects of the molecule as it interacts with my cells, is not trivial.

When repeated doses of an apolar compound accumulate in our system, a variety of unpredictable effects on cell membranes can be expected. It is not surprising, therefore, that the medical literature about amiodarone's use contains reports of diarrhea and changes in the permeability characteristics of intestinal epithelial cells, so they are not as effective in taking up—or may even begin to release—water and nutrients from digested food.

Then there are the nerve cells that send signals to other nerve or muscle cells over considerable distances. Those signals travel on extensions of the nerve cell called axons, which are insulated with multiple layers of axonal membranes (much as wires are covered by insulating materials in electrical circuits). If such membranes are altered, perhaps no longer insulated properly, the signals they transmit or the interactions among nerve cells in the brain might change. Perhaps this explains the nightmares and visual changes in people taking amiodarone.

The kidneys and liver process blood and remove molecular

waste material. They are thick with capillaries and heavily inundated with blood. It is not surprising that amiodarone may cause damage to both these organs when used for longer periods of time.

Within two weeks of starting the amiodarone protocol of 400 mg per day, I began to experience some of these symptoms. During this time, as I considered the points above, I read a few of the four thousand papers dealing with amiodarone. Cardiology groups published most; these papers described studies of ten or twenty patients who were treated with amiodarone and then compared to control groups (similar patients who were not so treated), reporting improved survival rates for those who had received amiodarone. This looked like success.

If one deals with patients in their mid or late seventies, this may well have been appropriate. Amiodarone deals effectively with these patients' tachycardia experience . . . and does it better than with any of the alternative drugs. Side effects may be less important to older patients (and their caretakers) than the positive effects of reducing the incidence or intensity of tachycardia events.

• • •

When Bernie first experienced episodes of ventricular tachycardia (VT) in 1999, cardiologists knew very little about what initiated VT episodes, how they became sustained, or what to do to control them. We did know that, for patients with seriously reduced pump function, the drugs studied for control of VT (other than amiodarone) had caused more deaths than they had prevented. At that time, Bernie did not have seriously reduced heart function, but this was still a worry. If the initial strategy for Bernie was going to be drug treatment, then amiodarone was a relatively safe choice. The operative term is "relatively."

The appearance of relative safety came from the fact that, because of their advanced heart disease, patients who received amiodarone for VT usually didn't live long enough to experience its long-term side effects. In fact, in an attempt to be entirely honest with my patients, I told many of them, "If you live long enough to have long-term side effects, your treatment will have been successful."

• • •

But after I had looked at the chemical structure of amiodarone, it looked a lot less friendly to me than it looked to the cardiologists. I kept notes on what I experienced and learned after the first few weeks of amiodarone usage. As I said, I found about four thousand papers by medical practitioners. I also searched for work on amiodarone by chemists, and I discovered about forty papers. The ratio of 1 to 100 for chemical studies versus clinical studies suggested to me the possibility that the medical community might not appreciate some of the points about the general effects of polar (water-soluble) versus non–polar drugs.

• • •

Amiodarone is a very strange drug indeed, and it has been studied extensively since the early 1960s. It has an unusual chemical structure with high iodine content, and it is not very soluble in water. Most importantly, when Bernie started taking amiodarone, its mechanism of action (the exact how and why it works to suppress heart rhythm disorder) remained unknown.

• • •

I wrote a five-page summary of these likely effects for Dr. Candinas. My summary included a few sketches of structures and membranes to clarify these points. I concluded that I saw little to be gained by taking amiodarone and going through a second electrophysiological exam, which would undoubtedly produce the expected result (namely, the maximum heart rate during tachycardia would be lower, perhaps significantly lower).

I would not collapse due to the occasional tachycardia. But with the continued accumulation of amiodarone, I could imagine that my innards would gradually waste away . . . as might my mind and certainly my not-all-that-acute eyesight. So I wrote my little note for Dr. Candinas. He was, like most of his colleagues, aware of the side effects of this drug, but what to do when nothing else looks any better?

• • •

Bernie had a good point in voicing his concerns about the issue of long-term side effects. Amiodarone can cause serious lung and liver problems, and after a year or two of taking it, many patients develop a strange blue discoloration of the skin.

• • •

Ten minutes after I sent my note to Dr. Candinas, he called, agreed we should stop the amiodarone experiment, and announced he had cancelled the planned follow-up electrophysiological examination.

• • •

Bernie was simply doing what he was trained to do, loved to do, and spent his life doing. He was, above all, a scientist. He looked for information, found it, and processed it. As a patient, he was going to ask a lot of questions. Something about amiodarone triggered a strong response from Bernie. This chapter has some of his typically Dutch cultural slant on life: "What to do when nothing else looks any better?"

How many patients send a five-page report with figures and references to explain their reluctance to follow a recommended treatment?

Intellectually, Bernie did not agree with the plan. Physically, he continued to experience more symptoms. He soon found himself in a depressing dilemma.

• • •

During a recent walk, I was thinking of my heart and telling myself stories relating to my health, when it occurred to me that a book about my heart would allow me to deal with many of my favorite topics. This might become a book reminiscent of *Zen and the Art of Motorcycle Maintenance,*[7] with factual information about the body and heart and more general interactions with our physical and mental environments. Titles suggested themselves: "My Heart and I" or "My Heart, That Beautiful Machine."

• • •

For readers who are not familiar with Zen and the Art of Motorcycle Maintenance: An Inquiry into Values, *Bernie's example for the sort of book he wanted to write reveals the depth of his distress.*

---

7   *Zen and the Art of Motorcycle Maintenance: An Inquiry into Values* by Robert M. Pirsig. William Morrow and Company, Inc., 1974. New York

When Robert Pirsig, the author of Zen *(Vitello, 2017), died, his obituary in* The New York Times *quoted sociologist Todd Gitlin's description of the book: "[S]eeking to reconcile humanism with technological progress, . . . perfectly timed for a generation weary of the '60s revolt against a soulless high-tech world dominated by a corporate and military-industrial order.*

"There is such a thing as a zeitgeist," Gitlin continued, "and I believe the book was popular because there were a lot of people who wanted a reconciliation—even if they didn't know what they were looking for. Pirsig provided a kind of soft landing from the euphoric stratosphere of the late '60s into the real world of adult life."[8]

Our generation—Bernie's and mine—understood the importance of making that "soft landing."

• • •

On another note, I have been rowing every other day, with mixed results. I was moving up on total rowing time (four sets of eleven minutes, mostly around 3:10 for 500 meters—not much but a lot better than nothing), but lately, I have run into unstable heart rhythms after only two sets. In addition, I am feeling occasional dull pains (minor but obvious enough) in my left lower chest and some pressure in my upper chest area.

Ton [Renske's brother] just had one of his arteries dilated with a stent, and this was precipitated by chest pains and difficulties keeping up on the hockey field. Now I am asking myself whether heart rhythm problems are my only issues. I should have a good examination of the physical state of my cardiovascular

---

8   https://www.nytimes.com/2017/04/24/books/robert-pirsig-dead-wrote-zen-and
    -the-art-of-motorcycle-maintenance.html

system to be sure that the mechanical part is fine and only its rhythm regulation needs improvement.

Adding all of this together, I am back to my normal state: a bit concerned about my laboratory and private finances; not too sure that any of my start-ups will go anywhere; mumbling about long-term plans for books and electric trees; seeing my colleagues perform with great energy and commitment; and dissatisfied about my present and probable future state.

And then there are patents. Patents will be a problem in everything I do. There is competition everywhere.

I will not be able to do things alone; with other people involved, things always get more complicated. So, the potential for a lot of interesting activity is there. It will be a lot of work, and that is just how it will always be.

· · ·

This is an uncharacteristically downbeat soliloquy. Bernie lived in a highly competitive world; like many other scientists working in biotechnology, he had an entrepreneurial streak. He had biotech start-up ventures in which patents were problematic and "competition everywhere." In addition, his rowing wasn't going well, and his brother-in-law had just undergone an emergency stenting procedure.

Accepting reality can be depressing. As he tried to come to terms with how to restructure his life to accommodate illness, he accepted the fact he needed some help. On the other hand, he preferred doing this himself. He needed to find a new balance to maintain his rowing, laboratory, and businesses, and doing so would be "a lot of work."

CHAPTER 4

240 BPM

Rowing holds a unique spot among team sports for its fundamental simplicity, sustained and intense physical demands on the oarsman, and absolute requirement of maximum effort.

Bernie continued to train, either rowing on the water or on his Concept2, a very high-quality indoor rowing machine used by enthusiasts for home training. He trained by following the same rules of scientific investigation learned in college biology: state the hypothesis, standardize the methods, collect the experimental data, and discuss the results.

His hypothesis was that certain activities would trigger unstable heart rates. So he came up with a method to monitor his heart rate. After he learned how to induce his arrhythmia, he presented his data for review.

Some people would say this was madness.

No. It was typical Bernie.

• • •

I bought a new monitor to check my heart rate from time to time. Runners and other athletes use them to track heart rate during exercise. Mine sensed heartbeats through two electrodes embedded in a chest belt strapped directly under the pectoral muscles (pecs). This puts the electrodes against the skin on either side of the sternum, about twenty centimeters (or eight inches) apart. The two electrodes pick up electrical heart beat impulses, just as happens when electrodes are attached to the skin when having an electrocardiogram (ECG) taken at the doctor's office or in the hospital. An ECG machine has ten electrodes connected by wires to a piece of equipment that records the signals and then produces paper graphs or shows results on a computer display. The signals coming from the chest belt with its two electrodes are transmitted to a receiver or monitor that usually looks like a wristwatch. Most of the time, this is enough to give an accurate heart rate. The monitor processes the information and displays the heartbeat in number of beats per minute or as a percentage of the wearer's maximum predicted heart rate

Various versions of these devices exist. Some store information during a training session; more high-end devices can also record air temperature and elevation. This information can be downloaded to a computer to generate graphs of heartbeat versus time, elevation, temperature, and even GPS location. A device for cyclists records information about the power generated by each leg during pedal rotations. Sprinters can record a preset sequence of sprints, warm-ups, and cooldowns.

The present uses of and potential for these devices are enormous. The different sorts of sensors that can be added to the menu is expanding. There is a small company in Zurich working with physiologists and sensor specialists to develop software that can follow ten or more parameters to provide information about an athlete's performance during training and competitions. These technologies will, of course, diffuse into the consumer market. This is the same way that Formula One racing generates better automobile components based on new materials and mountains of software. Within a few years, these improved components turn up in Porsches and high-end Mercedes-Benzes, BMWs, and Audis. The rest of the car world follows along in a few more years.

I continued doing the yoga-like exercises, which I often did before breakfast, and tried to continue jogging as I had done most of my life, all while wearing the monitor. But now I looked at what the heart rate monitor measured as I exercised. I exerted myself against common sense and my wife's advice, as well as those friends whom I'd told about the activities. I suppose I did it because physical activity had always helped in the past. This time, however, the news was not good.

When I put on my running gear and walked out of the house for my standard five kilometer route in the woods, the monitor showed a reasonable 65 or 70 bpm. Nothing much happened during the first few minutes of jogging, but then my heart rate would often suddenly go from 70 to 110 or 120 bpm. A minute later, it might drop back down to 80 bpm and then follow a steadily increasing rate. After another four or five minutes, when I would encounter a moderate uphill stretch rising twenty or so meters, I would sometimes experience a tachycardia, my wrist monitor showing 240 bpm.

I came to dislike and fear 240 bpm. I could see it coming, as the rate on the monitor suddenly and rapidly climbed. Accompanying the rising rate was an odd and unpleasant sensation, a kind of breathlessness, and a feeling of emptiness in my chest.

I knew, of course, that it wasn't wise to allow these tachycardia to happen. I had read about their effects on older people who often collapsed and, in a number of cases, did not survive more than two or three of these events. I was not trying to be a sort of hero, immune to all that we experience as we age. However, I didn't think these tachycardia would kill me. They were unpleasant. I was immobilized. I just had to wait until they passed, although this often took several hours. Interesting thoughts.

Reality looked different.

During that first year, I experienced at least ten tachycardia lasting two hours or more and ended up in Zurich University Hospital's intensive care unit a few more times for overnight treatments.

Toward the end of that year, I made my way home with one of these 240 bpm tachycardia. Tired of impromptu visits to the hospital, I sank down on a couch for seven or eight hours. My Polar heart rate monitor was showing a steady 240 bpm, but I made my way to the kitchen for an occasional glass of water and even a bowl of yogurt. I concluded that my heart could handle this lengthening time, beating away at two to four times its normal pace. My heart was like an engine that's not in gear and running wild.

My wife came home and took me to the intensive care unit, but I could have called an ambulance.

I could have called a taxi!

I don't know why I didn't call. I do remember feeling a little sorry for myself; I was probably trying to make my wife feel guilty, although I'm not sure why.

I continued doing my morning exercises, often daily, sometimes every other day. These, too, I did with the heart rate monitor. It can show heart rate as a number or as individual blips visible on the little screen or as an audible beat: *beep-beep-beep* . . .

My exercise typically consisted of limbering-up sequences: standing, arms extending up, down, forward, back and sideways; knee bends, crouching, lying on my back, sides, prone; lifting legs. I based most of this on a few standard yoga sequences. My heart rate rarely exceeded 100 bpm during three twelve-to-fifteen-minute sets. I usually followed this with several sets of sit-ups and push-ups, with a resulting heart rate of 110 to 125 bpm toward the end.

After exercising for a while and listening to the *beep-beep-beep* of my monitor, I noticed that the beating patterns were not the same. When I went through the same movements on the right side of my body, I compared the patterns to the left side. When I lay extended on my left side and raised my right leg five times, for example, the *beep-beep-beep* pattern sounded different from what I heard when I lay on my right side and lifted my left leg five times.

I took care to make the movements as similar as I could: legs nearly straight, elevation to about fifty degrees horizontal, legs extended in line with my upper body lying on the floor. Clearly, the position of my heart and the effects of the muscles involved in raising an extended leg from the horizontal were not the same for my two sides. I concluded that the physical position of my heart within my chest had some effect on the regulation of my heartbeat.

Another interesting effect was clearly noticeable during sit-ups. Starting from a horizontal position on the floor, I would hear a nice regular beat (usually around 80 bpm) at the beginning of a set. As my upper body rose, hands at my neck, I would hear a sudden rapid *ta-ta-ta*, much faster than the 80 bpm while I was lying relaxed and flat on the floor. As my upper body went through the vertical towards my legs, the *ta-ta-ta* disappeared and beeps returned to a rate similar to what I'd heard when I lay flat. The same pattern recurred with every sit-up, telling me that my chest's compression as I became more vertical affected my heart in some way such as to significantly increase the triggering rate.

Push-ups also involve compression of the chest when one's

extended body is pushed away from the floor. Doing push-ups also caused a rapid rise of my heart rate, although it was less clear whether this was due to the specifics of the chest compression or greater effort.

That the heart is suspended by various surrounding tissues and connecting arteries and veins seemed obvious to me. It is hard to imagine that it would occupy precisely the same space with precisely the same interactions as we stand; lie down; sit; lean forward, backward, or sideways; roll; jump or run around or are jumped on; fall; or walk into objects. In short, our internal organs are not immobile.

Possibly, all these movements and shocks affect regulation of our heart rates. That being the case, I expected a simple search to uncover a general awareness of this and significant literature describing the phenomenon and its implications. In 1999, my first forays into this presumed literature did not produce any results. I may not have looked long enough or in the best places, so I also consulted some of my friends in the sector.

A number of my college classmates went into medicine, including cardiology. Some of my good friends are members of medical school faculties in the US, and a number of my former PhD students are professors in medical schools in the Netherlands. My Institute of Biotechnology was one of six in ETH Zurich's biology department, and several colleagues from the medical school and hospital of the University of Zurich (the same place where, in 1999, I ended up in the intensive care unit from time to time) were on the faculty. And then, there were my heart rhythm specialist and his colleagues in the Department of Cardiology in this same medical school and hospital of the University of Zurich.

None of the people I consulted recognized the effects I reported.

A few of my very good friends—very able clinicians—suggested that I measured too much. My wife and close family shared this feeling, and it was probably true.

Still, I could not believe that NASA, with its astronauts spinning around at 5 or 6 G's, hadn't looked at this. If the heart rate is influenced, at least in some situations, by its position and local pressures, it might have been seen in centrifuge experiments. My friends, however, had never heard of such experiments or results.

After I stopped taking amiodarone, life gradually became more difficult. I experienced tachycardia on various occasions: during dinner with Arian van Vemde, a good friend, at the neighboring hotel, the Grand Dolder; during attempts to jog in the woods around our home; during one of Jay's student's PhD exam while I tried to concentrate on the questions I planned to bring up; during walks with my wife; at home sometimes; during jogs in Maine while visiting my daughter, Anna; during a walk with Wout [another brother] in Springfield, Massachusetts; during jogs in California while visiting Gjalt Huisman; after a lecture at Maxygen.

Sometimes I visited Dr. Candinas, my heart rhythm specialist, to discuss these happenings. One day, he suggested I follow my heart rate for twenty-four hours by wearing a Holter monitor.[9] I went through my normal daily routine for the first twenty-two hours. During the last two, I did the exercises I knew would cause an increased heart rate pattern: sit-ups, lying on one side or another and raising an extended leg, push-ups, and so on.

I returned the Holter monitor to the clinic. A few hours later, Dr. Candinas called to tell me that everything looked fine during most of the recording, but the reading was quite chaotic toward

9   A wearable device that records a continuous electrocardiogram for twenty-four to seventy-two hours. The name honors one of its two inventors, Norman Holter (the other was Wilford Glasscock).

the end. "I know," I told him. "I went through various movements and positions to cause that."

"Hmm ... " he responded. "Can you reproduce that? Can you do these exercises here while we measure your heart performance?"

A few days later, I was lying on the floor at the clinic, with Dr. Candinas facing his equipment. I announced what I expected my heart rate to do during the next set of movements and then went through them. I watched Dr. Candinas's back as he stared at his monitor. After thirty or forty minutes, he turned around, looked at me, and announced: "*Sie haben es objektiviert*" ("You have objectified it"). A better translation might be "OK, so the observations you have been talking about can actually be observed with my equipment as well as with your Polar heart rate monitor."

Before I moved to Zurich, I had always thought English was a very efficient and rather precise language. German usually required more words to convey the same thoughts. But about half of the biology professors at ETH Zurich were Germans, and I had learned in our department meetings that German, spoken by good native speakers, was in fact very precise and elegant—a joy to listen to.

Anyway, it was now a respectable notion that hearts, or at least my heart, did beat irregularly when bodies, or my body in any case, went through various contortions. I went home, life went on, and there were no particular consequences. The tachycardia kept coming, more rather than less.

• • •

Patients' use of denial as a psychological defense mechanism baffles physicians.
Patients, however, seem very comfortable with it. When I have asked

patients directly about this, they generally say something along the lines of "Of course I'm in denial. How else would I get anything done?"

At this stage in his relationship with his own heart, denial was extremely useful for Bernie. With denial, he could maintain some sort of life. If he had been objective, he would have admitted that he was almost sixty years of age and qualified as one of those older patients who might well die during a VT episode. Nonetheless, as he said, "I did not think that these tachycardia would kill me."

Well, Bernie—that qualifies as denial.

More importantly, instead of feeling fearful when he eventually learned how to trigger his episodes, he wanted to demonstrate to Dr. Candinas that he had gained some degree of control over his condition.

I empathize with Bernie's electrophysiologist. This must have been a challenging period in the evolution of their doctor–patient relationship. Watching his patient, a highly productive scientist, teacher, and entrepreneur, demonstrate his unsupervised self-induction of VT episodes must have been like watching Bernie play Russian roulette!

Yet our job as physicians is to help our patients live as fully as possible.

How do doctors deal with this? How should we deal with it? We cannot avoid feeling some element of responsibility, but we cannot put ourselves in loco parentis or alienate our patients by trying to forbid some activity or another. We do not, after all, have that kind of power.

We are advisors. After too many years, and too many mistakes, I believe that the reasonable middle ground is to have an honest conversation with patients, preferably including their spouses (and then document the outcomes in the record!). In that discussion, the physician should make every effort to report the medical facts and describe the foreseeable consequences of the available management options. As long as individual patients are mentally competent, the decision of what risks are acceptable is theirs.

CHAPTER 5

D-o-o-o-i-i-i-n-n-n-k-k-k!

It was 1999.

After we had given up on amiodarone, I lived without any medication; I don't recall exactly why. I focused on using my morning exercise routine, along with walking, jogging, and swimming, to try to find my old self. This had always worked in the past, but not this time. My heart rhythm specialist still felt that I should seriously consider having an ICD installed.

"This is the gold standard," Dr. Candinas said. "It is time to take this step."

I was not yet ready for that, and so I accepted the occasional tachycardia as a new fact of life.

•••

In the late 1950s, pioneering physicians like Paul Zoll in Boston began to study the clinical effects of electrical stimuli applied to the heart. His work culminated in the development of an effective external defibrillator, and the availability of this technology subsequently led to the introduction of the first coronary care units (CCUs) in 1962. The coronary care experience quickly demonstrated that VT was a frequent cause of death after heart attacks and that prompt electrical defibrillation could be lifesaving.

Beginning in 1969, Michael Mirowski, a Polish émigré and physician who had taken a position as the director of the coronary care unit at Sinai Hospital in Baltimore, worked for over a decade to develop a battery-powered defibrillator suitable for clinical use; the device could be implanted in patients at risk for death due to VT. Thanks to Mirowski's vision and persistence, the first successful ICD implantation in a human was performed in February 1980, and thousands of lives have been saved since.[10]

As the field advanced, the devices became smaller and more reliable; the batteries lasted longer, and ICDs became the accepted treatment for many patients, including those like Bernie, with preserved pumping function and conditions that predispose to ventricular arrhythmias.

The heart rhythm specialist's recommendation made sense.

• • •

In the summer, Renske and I traveled to New England, visiting family and attending a conference. In Maine, we saw Anna, my daughter, and my jogging resulted in one or two tachycardia. I felt them, stopped running, and was not very happy.

A few days later in Springfield, my brother invited me to join him on a fund-raising hike in support of hungry children somewhere. It was really just a walk, but when I tried to overtake a few elderly people, I saw "240" appear on the monitor. I ended up sitting under a tree while solicitous policemen suggested taking me to Springfield General Hospital.

I did not look forward to going into an emergency room (I might have a difficult time escaping), so the officers agreed to take

---

10   Marc W. Deyell, MD, FRCPC; Stanley Tung, MD, FRCPC; Andrew Ignaszewski, MD, FRCPC; "The implantable cardioverter-defibrillator: From Mirowski to its current use." *British Columbia Medical Journal* 52, no. 5 (June 2010): 248

us home. After a while, the tachycardia ended. Having it vanish, with a nice 90, then 80 bpm, was always a fine moment. Life seemed a lot more livable, if only until the next event.

As the fall of 1999 wore on, I slowed down. I had more difficulty keeping up with other people while walking in the woods. I spent more time than ever before just catching my breath after going up a few steps on the stairs. Life was not much fun anymore. My family felt I should stop working full time; "Go to half time to get enough rest," they said. In my practice, I was already working half time but it took me full time to do it.

My wife began talking about a wheelchair.

I knew, or believed, that none of their suggestions would do any good. Reducing my activity further would simply accelerate whatever process I was experiencing; it would slow me down even more with no help in sight. That year, after my first visit in February, I ended up in the intensive care unit on three more nights. After each of these events, I spent some time with Dr. Candinas, and each time, he advised me to get an ICD. Toward the end of the year, I could see no other way out. In January 2000, it was done.

• • •

Finally! Although generally bright and competent, Bernie could be a bit stubborn. Clearly, 1999 had been a miserable year for him.

• • •

A modern ICD can be programmed and interrogated after it has been implanted using an electronic device (called a programmer) that communicates with the ICD through the skin, almost like a Bluetooth device. My new ICD recorded each heartbeat and stored the most recent thousand beats in its memory. This electro-cardiographic memory is useful.

If my ICD delivered a shock to end a tachycardia, then the electrophysiologist could interrogate its memory to look at the heart rhythm that prompted the shock. The electrophysiologist usually sets the device to deliver shocks in a series of steps. Typically, it might come into action when it sees a ten or fifteen heartbeat rise above 160 bpm. The first step is to charge a capacitor,[11] which can then deliver a shock to the heart chambers from electrodes that connect the ICD to the atrium, ventricle, or both.

The ICD can be programmed to vary the electrical intensity of the delivered shocks. The device will initiate a protocol to deliver a low-power shock of 6 Joules,[12] which can be carried out twice. If this does not work, the device goes on to another shock, now of intermediate power, repeated if need be. If that does not work, the device goes to a maximum power shock, which is also repeated if the first does not work.

On the day after I returned home, I went for a walk with my wife. There were a few ups and downs on the route. "Ups and downs" are basically unavoidable in Switzerland, unless one walks along one of the many lakes' shores. About thirty minutes after leaving the house, my ICD came to life, and I experienced the first of its jolts. I needed the maximum power shock, which one can very clearly feel.

I sat down for a while before continuing, only to have another shock as we walked home.

---

11 A capacitor can store an electric charge and then release all the stored energy very quickly.

12 A Joule is a unit of electrical energy.

Renske and I tried again the following day, and despite my attempts to be conservative in what I did, I experienced two shocks, much like the previous day. After that, I became more careful.

The net effect was that I probably did even less than before I had the ICD.

That was when I realized that the device had not cured whatever was wrong in my heart. The ICD basically provided a safety line. When you go climbing in the mountains, wearing a safety line does not prevent you from slipping, losing your footing, or falling. It simply keeps the fall from turning into a major disaster. So it is with the ICD. It changes nothing about the problem triggering abnormal heartbeats. However, if the heart rhythm goes outside the specific programmed boundaries, the device will keep you from falling off the cliff. Without it, and with no access to a nearby emergency room or automated external defibrillator (AED) device at an airport or other public place, there is nothing that can return your heart rate to normal.

In addition, the functionality of these devices is limited by their batteries. The battery lasts four to six years, at most. The number of shocks that the battery can deliver depends on the electrical energy required to actually stop a tachycardia. If the maximum energy, nearly 20 Joules, is required each time a tachycardia occurs, then the ICD can only produce about ten large shocks each year if it is going to last five years. A continuous process of heart rate regulation, where every little tachycardia is eliminated within a few minutes and the user lives a normal life, is not possible.

All of this discussion assumes that the wearer will have no problems, either physiologically or psychologically, with experiencing frequent shocks to terminate tachycardia. However, at the best, many people with an ICD dislike the shocks the device produces; at worst, they come to fear them. I was told about one patient who, after his first ICD shock, returned to the hospital to have the device removed immediately.

I would not go that far, but the shocks are unpleasant. They felt as if I were hitting a very solid tree stump with a dull ax or large sledgehammer. The hit reverberates back into your body through the arms and shoulders, with a sort of *D-o-o-o-i-i-i-n-n-n-k-k-k!*

But the ICD shock happens directly inside your heart.

So, the ICD does not and cannot solve the primary problem, which is that something is wrong with the regulation of the heart rate.

• • •

This sad, but true, insight came early for Bernie. Many patients undergo device implantation and then don't experience a shock for months, or even years.

• • •

My life became progressively more difficult. After I walked to the kitchen to make a cup of tea (about fifteen meters and without any stairs), I would stand panting while I put the water on to boil. I could still drive to the lab, but the walk from the garage involving climbing two sets of stairs had become a major hurdle. Once in the Institute, walking down the hall to my office required at least one pause to lean, hopefully nonchalantly, against a wall. Of course, I fooled no one. Teaching, with occasional two-hour lectures, was no longer effortless.

I continued walking around the woods, but my routes were now modest stretches without hills. Octogenarians easily overtook me. Functionally, I was becoming a nonagenarian in advance of my sixtieth birthday.

What would happen next? I had lost my capacity to look forward to—and even my ability to imagine—future events. I had no ability to plan a little with others.

As I tried to understand this, it dawned on me that to look forward, make plans, and hope for something, one has to be able to believe the future can happen. Once one knows it cannot, imagining and planning become a fantasy, a mirage, and can no longer be taken seriously.

• • •

With his comment that "Planning for the future requires belief that the future will happen," Bernie shares a deep and troubling insight. When faced with a serious illness, all of us truly need to believe in a realizable future. With our focus on the immediate problem of helping patients live with disease, we physicians often fail to communicate our belief that the patient's future will actually happen.

In my own practice experience, I slowly realized that the simple act of scheduling a return visit could play a critical role in the management of chronic disease. Simply saying "I will see you in six months" communicates the assurance that the physician expects a future for the patient, and the physician fully intends to participate in that future by providing continuing care.

• • •

I cannot recall what the specific reason was for once again seeing Dr. Candinas, my heart rhythm specialist, but there we were. I told him something had to happen. There had to be an alternative medication to amiodarone, which I still did not consider an option. There had to be something more than the ICD. Perhaps the device was the gold standard, but it alone was not sufficient, not for a fifty-nine-year-old who still wanted to be active.

"What would you suggest?" he enquired, doubtless mindful of my reaction to his amiodarone prescription.

"The best you have to offer," I responded, desperate for impossible magic.

"It is all trial and error," said Dr. Candinas.

"Yes, your trial, my error . . . " I ventured, and we laughed a little—he more than I, perhaps.

"Ah, medicine. A beautiful occupation, were it not for the patients," sighed my specialist.

I could only agree, since my laboratory bacteria never complained. They simply kept on doing what they were fated to do. It was up to us to understand them a little, but we had plenty of time and no one worried about a few bacteria more or less at the end of a day of experiments.

"Maybe we should try flecainide," he continued.

"What is that?"

"Similar to amiodarone but not used as much. It can be toxic at relatively low dosages. And we should combine it with a beta blocker, like metoprolol succinate." he said.

• • •

With the ICD device in place, Dr. Candinas was willing to consider a drug program of flecainide and metoprolol succinate, attempting to suppress the lesser episodes with drugs that are less effective than amiodarone but better tolerated.

...

I took his prescriptions, bought the new drugs, and made preparations for a trip with my wife to Edinburgh the following day.
I was scheduled to give a lecture there. Afterward, we would stay
for the Theatre and Arts Festival and then travel around Scotland.

In Edinburgh, we took a short walk and ran into Lex de
Lange, one of my friends from Groningen. He was the director
of the science park there, which several people and I had set up
in the 1980s, and Lex had worked hard to make something of
it. Lex was a big fellow, a high voltage extrovert who was somehow always surrounded by a bunch of even bigger and rather
tough-looking Groningeners who had various functions related
to the science park or Lex's various projects. They were most
definitely not your typical academics, but I knew some of them
and they were just lovely people. Inevitably, there were big plans:
an expanding empire with new science parks here and there—
Poland, Australia, the UK, Germany—usually with a shortage of
funds, but this was to be solved soon. There was the usual banter,
a lot of laughter, a few beers, and an occasional cigar. My wife and
I joined them in one of Edinburgh's bars, and I quickly forgot all
about my generally feeble state.

As I write about this, I realize how unbelievably important
it is to have good friends, to be able to simply have a good time.
And I can imagine what a disaster it would be to not have these
friends when one is hit by any of the many illnesses that come
along in life.

The following morning, I took my second doses of flecainide
and metoprolol succinate. Then we went out for a short walk.
We soon encountered a slight slope. I had become careful about

when and where I walked. I was very aware of small obstacles and looked for driveways when crossing a street in order not to have to step down from or up to the sidewalk. I had to pay attention to where my feet landed to keep my equilibrium. In short, I was your typical ninety-year-old, venturing out for a little life on the street.

As we began to walk up the modest grade, I waited for the usual out-of-breath-and-empty-chest sensation that usually forced me to stop for a break after thirty or forty meters before continuing. Where was it? I walked well beyond those forty meters and continued on. And on ... we were now walking up the slope ... What was happening? What was this?

We reached the highest point of the route. I looked back. We had covered perhaps three hundred meters, including "climbing" ten or fifteen meters. It would have been nothing two years earlier, but this was a major achievement now. Life came flowing back into me, an avalanche. I did not yet dare to trust this. It was an oddity perhaps; maybe something about Edinburgh. But also, it carried a delicious feeling of promise: still early, fragile, but yet ...

We travelled to Fort Williams, a tiny village on the west coast of Scotland with beautiful wind-sculpted hills—tan like the northern California hills adjacent to the Pacific. We found a little hotel and went for another walk, quite level. We walked on and on, worrying a little about the return; better not to push this new gift. In the end, we probably covered five or six kilometers. Life was really coming back!

Back in Zurich, I looked into flecainide. The molecule is smaller than amiodarone and much more water-soluble. It was usually prescribed at 200 to 400 mg per day. As Dr. Candinas had said, there were concerns about its effects at higher doses, and practitioners looked at flecainide with significant reservations. I suspected that I might end up using this compound for the rest of my life, possibly twenty to thirty years, perhaps even longer. My body might undergo some adaptation during such a long period and need progressively more of the drug to achieve the same effect. In order to mitigate this potential risk, I decided to use the minimum amount that would give me the desired effect today. I cut my dose back from 200 to 100 mg per day.

I also halved the metoprolol succinate dose, from 50 to 25 mg per day.

• • •

Once again, Bernie could not resist tinkering with the doses. There was a distinct and irritating undercurrent of hubris in this. He altered his drug doses, offering the rationale that he might "become resistant" in the future.

I have had some patients who did this. I felt conflicted, angry, and frustrated whenever I found out about it. Why should a patient bother to take an ineffective dose? Even more troubling, reduction in doses can be a route to incurring the risks of adverse effects, which are often not dose-related, without getting the dose-dependent potential therapeutic benefit.

On the other hand, perhaps taking some medication is preferable to none?

• • •

It was now mid-2000.

I was totally out of shape, pale, with flaccid hair falling over my forehead. A single glass of wine made me feel queasy, even a little nauseous.

I began to rebuild my body. I started the morning exercises once again and walked progressively more. I continued to measure my heart rate with the Polar heart rate monitor while I tried to distinguish various patterns. I began to see the relationship between certain sensations and the heart rate patterns shown by the Polar device. A stable heart rate felt comfortable. When the monitor showed repeated abrupt transitions from 70 to 100 bpm (or more) and then back down, I felt an unpleasant, unstable sensation.

My heart skipped beats with great frequency. I could easily follow this at night while lying in bed and feeling the sensation of my heartbeat or by taking my pulse at various arteries: the carotids (along the neck) and the large arteries (those feeding the legs or even around the ankles).

Each told the same tale. Though about every third or fourth beat was lost, nothing strange seemed to happen. I would have preferred to feel a regular beat, but I was not at all sure whether this was critical or important in any way. Whether the beats are regular or not, blood will be pumped through the lungs and into all of the body—or so I told myself.

· · ·

Over years of talking with patients, I have heard this description of night-time awareness of arrhythmia from countless patients. Two phenomena are probably involved. First, the heart rate tends to increase with activity, and the higher rates tend to "overdrive suppress" the irregular beats.[13] Because of this overdrive suppression, many patients don't notice arrhythmias as much when they are moderately active. Second, and even more important, activity draws attention away from the internal world of the body to the outside world. But when lying in bed, quiet, alone in one's own skin, the temptation to monitor heartbeats becomes irresistible.

---

13   With an increase in normal heart rate, time available for abnormal beats to occur
     decreases. Thus, activity suppresses the irregular beats.

. . .

As I started walking again, trying to do three, four, or five stretches of five hundred meters or so at a time, I seemed to see improvement. But it was all awfully slow. Still, it was immensely better than it had been before the flecainide, when my capabilities were dwindling towards zero.

I noticed various symptoms. I felt unsteady and had to pay attention to how I walked. My gait had changed: I tended to walk with my legs slightly farther apart, each foot tracing a line that moved farther apart, apparently because my body was trying not to fall over. Inserting a key into a lock took more concentration and effort because my hand needed to search a little longer to line the key up with the lock.

Occasionally, my cheeks would tighten up around the cheekbones and then my field of vision would shrink—not too much but noticeably. Sometimes my shoulders and upper arms would feel sore and weak. I interpreted these happenings as effects of reduced blood flow in the affected areas.

Drinking wine was not very pleasant; neither were my sporadic attempts to smoke a cigar. These activities still made me feel a little nauseous, a little ill.

I felt uncertain driving a car. Going into a tunnel was unpleasant. When I'd look sideways toward a passing car, that sudden, fast movement would cause a slight sensation of vertigo. I began to worry about my chances of ending up in an accident and the risk of harming myself and others.

My functioning oscillated back and forth between *unstable* and *just fine*. I travelled to Venice to teach chemistry graduate students in a summer school organized by one of my Italian colleagues. One evening, I was walking along one of the many canals. Everything had seemed in order until suddenly, I began to feel unstable. I found it difficult not to veer toward the water, so I squeezed against walls. I made my way toward any shop that might serve food, especially sweets. I found a suitable place, had a generous helping of ice cream and cake, and walked away much happier than when I'd entered.

The following day, I was in fine shape. I had dinner with a friend and afterward, when we had to move speedily in the rain, I positively enjoyed dashing from awning to awning and across Venetian squares in the warm summer evening.

Basically, my situation seemed unreliable. I could not count on my ability to function to any extent, even with treatment.

• • •

Bernie's hopes for a cure were raised and then dashed. He accepted the heart rhythm specialist's recommendation for implantation of an ICD and then had to deal with the outcome. He soon realized that, though the device could effectively terminate his tachycardia episodes, this correction came at the very real cost of an unpleasant electrical shock. It became clear to Bernie that the ICD might prevent potentially fatal episodes, but it certainly wasn't a cure.

Medically managing chronic problems inevitably involves trade-offs: "We can do this, but it has a downside of that." Communication between doctors and patients is always colored by the doctor's beliefs and patient's hopes. The doctor's side of the conversation should be, "I can offer you this treatment, but even if it works, it has a downside. Can you handle that?"

CHAPTER 6

Magical, Wouldn't You Say?

After realizing his ICD represented a management tactic, not a cure, and medication provided limited efficacy, Bernie began thinking about his physical problems more broadly. He tried to frame an intellectual context in which he could deal with his situation.

This chapter presents two essays Bernie wrote about the heart. It's important to remember that, during his graduate school years at Hopkins, Bernie roomed with Tom Jacobs, an Amherst classmate and medical student who became a professor of medicine and award-winning teacher at Columbia University. There's no question: Through his associations, Bernie had been exposed to more human anatomy and physiology than the average microbiologist.

In this first essay, Bernie reviews how the heart, lungs, and metabolic needs of the body interact.

I've read this piece many times. Each time, I can hear Bernie's voice and see his eyebrows rise with his pitch, and he smiles as he remarks on some particularly fascinating point.

• • •

ESSAY

Blood carries everything our tissues need: oxygen, energy-rich sugars and fats, and the compounds needed to build the large molecules that go into the structure, repair, and maintenance of all of our cells. The body, this unbelievably complex machine, must not only be built and maintained but must also function continuously—preferably properly—every day of our lives.

Our bodies generate wastes. We have gas exchange in the lungs, which take in air, extract the oxygen, and pass it to the blood, which then takes it to all of our cells. Each cell pushes out carbon dioxide that is returned to the lungs, where it is transferred into the air that we then expel. And we have kidneys that filter the blood and regulate its composition.

Magical, wouldn't you say? And yet, thus far, only a structure has been built; or better yet, a structure has been *described;* this is biochemistry as accounting.

• • •

For the casual reader, that last line is an experimentalist looking down his nose at observational science. Bernie's whole scientific life revolved around planning and doing experiments in the lab. People like me, whose work includes the occasional case report or epidemiologic observation, hold only second-class citizenship in the rarified world of academics.

• • •

Structure must function—and for many years. There are solutions for these problems; our bodies have all sorts of glands that produce molecules to keep everything in appropriate balance during every single day, with its light and dark diurnal rhythms, changing seasons, and various stages of life.

Then we have our neural systems, with sensors scanning the environment and integrators weighing all of these inputs and producing outputs that are, hopefully, appropriate. These systems' evolution has led to developing the brains we have today. Our brains deal not only with input of the present but with the past, future, and sometimes even the unseen, unheard, untasted, unsmelled, and unfelt (in a word, *imagined*).

The organism must also see to it that when gone, others will be there to follow. What is more, the organism must function in close interaction with a few or many of its kind. They affect one another more or less, depending on their numbers and proximity.

That Heart . . .

So, here is that little heart, about the size of a softball. The heart consists of four chambers: the left and right ventricles, at the bottom of the heart, and the left and right atria, on top of the ventricles. The walls of these chambers are basically muscle tissue.

Weighing about three-hundred grams (ten ounces), the heart's four chambers are tasked with getting blood to our bodies' every single living cell—around a hundred trillion of them, give or take a few trillion. Some of those cells need only a little blood flow; others, always busy, need more.

All of this blood pumping is powered by the left ventricle. The ventricle has a volume of around 100 ml (a little more than 3 ounces) and about 70 percent of this is expelled with each beat. The ventricle is filled from the left atrium, the heart chamber immediately above that collects blood flow from the lungs.

The left atrial filling is really important. As we will see a little farther on, the real problem with maintaining blood flow when your heart rate is that 240 bpm is that it allows adequate time to empty the left ventricle but inadequate time to fill it.

At rest, adult people have heart rates of 60 to 70 bpm. This means that, when we are at rest, the left ventricle pushes out about 70 ml (2.4 ounces) of blood per beat, and it does this sixty, seventy, or eighty times per minute—more when awake and less when sleeping. Let's just say that we pump at least five liters of blood into our arterial system every single minute. This amounts to 300 liters per hour; 7,200 liters per day; 220,000 per month; 2,400,000 per year; and around 200,000,000 liters in a lifetime. This blood has a total mass of more than 200,000 metric tons (220,000 tons), more than the largest aircraft carrier or cruise ship in existence.

. . .

Sorry, Bernie, but there are now a couple of cruise ships operating in the 220,000-ton range, and an even larger one is in the works. This update does not, however, detract from the remarkable long-term performance of the heart.

. . .

A lifetime is a long time. Moving this volume is a very impressive accomplishment for a little muscle structure with an internal volume of about half a cup. The heart does its work without interruption and generally without much complaint for the first fifty years of existence. Have we humans ever produced a similar gadget with these performance characteristics?

Lungs

Our lungs take care of both filtering and gas exchange. Blood loaded with carbon dioxide and containing very little oxygen is channeled to the right atrium and then into the right ventricle, which pumps this blood into the lungs. The blood travels through large blood vessels that branch into ever more and ever smaller vessels, finally reaching the capillaries of the alveoli. These alveoli are specialized air-space structures in the lungs where gas exchange takes place. Here, carbon dioxide diffuses from the blood through the alveoli's specialized membranes to then be exhaled, like a car's exhaust leaving its cylinders. At the same time and in the opposite direction, the high concentration of oxygen in inhaled air promotes oxygen diffusion across these same alveolar membranes and into the blood that then returns to the left atrium. From the left atrium, the blood flows into the left ventricle and is then pumped out into the aorta. Off it goes again to all of our cells.

Our body's gases enter and exit the blood only through the lungs: Oxygen is taken up and carbon dioxide is expelled. Other metabolic processes expel waste gases, some of which we mammals can smell on another's breath.

We might wonder whose interests this serves: the source, the receiver, or the population?

. . .

After this remarkable summary of physiology, Bernie went on to consider how regulation of the heart rate occurs. In this second essay, he referred to "nerve cells" or "neural tissue" in the heart. Conceptually, these terms worked for him, but anatomically, they're incorrect. In fact, the specialized conduction tissue in the heart consists of highly differentiated cardiac cells,

not nerve tissue. For the most part, I have edited out this modest miscon-
ception. Still, the reader can follow his reasoning without any difficulty.

...

ESSAY

How is heart rate regulated, and what causes changes in the normal resting heart rate?

The heart consists primarily of muscle tissue. Muscle contraction in the heart is triggered by signals produced by nerve cells
that together constitute an electrical system. This neuroelectrical
system runs along the inner surfaces of the atria and ventricles.
The normal signal starts at the sinoatrial (SA) node, located near
the top of the heart. Electrical activity spreads through the two
atria and then converges on the atrioventricular (AV) node that
sits at the intersection between the upper (atria) and lower (ventricles) chambers and between the left and right chambers. After
a momentary delay at the AV node, the signal then spreads to the
left and right ventricles via sets of cells that form special paths,
large bundle branches, and smaller fascicles—similar to wires conducting an electric current. Signals traveling along the specialized
tissue pathways stimulate the mechanical contraction of the muscle tissue, and so there is coordinated contraction: first, the atrial
chambers, which pump blood to fill the ventricles; second, the
ventricles into the lungs and the aorta; and then throughout the
body tissues and cells.

The SA node is the heart's drum major. It sets the tempo.
Sometimes the band is directed in a quick march; sometimes, it's
the slow tempo of the school song.

The rate at which the heart must pump to provide the oxygen and nutrients required by our tissues constantly varies: at rest or asleep or under various loads, such as when we walk upstairs, do heavy work, or are under stress. The SA node responds to messages from the brain and hormones in the blood to vary the heart rate as needed. At the same time, the conducting system must follow suit and transmit the signals to the muscles, so that the atria and ventricles are triggered properly and the heart's contraction is coordinated. All of this should happen once or more every second and should work well for eighty or ninety years.

In some cases, the signals that trigger our heartbeats are no longer delivered as they should be, or the conducting system along the atrial or ventricular walls goes awry. Atrial fibrillation, for instance, occurs when the atrial chambers are triggered irregularly and at rates that usually tend to be higher than normal. The heart's finely tuned responses to the body's demands break down. The ventricles either do not fill completely or become overfilled, and cardiac output decreases. Older individuals, many with high blood pressure or diabetes, often develop atrial fibrillation. It can be debilitating but, by itself, is not fatal.

Ventricular tachycardia is different. In VT, the signals that set the tempo originate in the ventricles, not the SA node.

• • •

It's as if a large section of the band—maybe all the brass and percussion—decide to march on their own, and the drum major is left with only a few clarinet players faithfully following the correct tempo.

• • •

The rate is usually steady but much higher than normal, some-where between 150 and 300 bpm.[14] The heart beats, but the ven-tricles do not have enough time to adequately fill with blood after ejecting their content into major arteries. Nor is there enough time for blood to flow to the heart itself. The net result: With VT, the heart's blood output decreases and so less blood arrives at tissues that require it, most importantly the heart and the brain.

How to Restore Normal Heart Rates?

Well, quite obviously, the heart's triggering has to be corrected and its conducting system functioning as it is meant to function to restore normal heart rates. How can we achieve these goals? The current medical approach is to try various medications and see which work best. Via much trial and error, this approach often results in something that is effective.

Another approach is conducting research directed at under-standing the details of how specific organs and tissues function. Research starts with small animals (usually rodents) that, more or less, resemble humans. Preliminary work is often done on mice because this is cheaper and more easily explained to a concerned public. As we get closer to understanding specific processes being studied, researches graduate to experimentation with larger crea-tures (like dogs) and, finally, to monkeys. Even then, we still do not necessarily know enough to be able to directly apply the presumed solutions to humans. So, ultimately, new procedures, protocols, and medications must eventually be tested in clinical trials with humans.

---

14   Although well-trained young athletes (for instance, crews rowing a racing shell over a typical 2 km Olympic distance) can manage "normal" heart rates of almost 200 bpm for several minutes, this is not desirable for untrained and older people.

• • •

Bernie and I discussed clinical research frequently. I spent much of my career involved in clinical trials. It's important for readers to understand that the FDA gives very clear guidance to researchers about informing patients who participate in such trials: "A clear statement that the clinical investigation involves research is important so prospective subjects are aware that, although preliminary data (bench, animal, pilot studies, literature) may exist, the purpose of their participation is primarily to contribute to research (for example, to evaluate the safety and effectiveness of the test article, to evaluate a different dose or route of administration of an approved drug, etc.) rather than to their own medical treatment."[15]

• • •

Finally, new proposed medications or devices are brought for review and potential approval to American and European agencies, such as the FDA or the European Medicines Agency (EMA) If approved, those medications and devices can then be used in medical practice.

Various medicines have been developed for cardiac arrhythmias, and they are in use with varying effects in individual patients. Catheter-based procedures to modify the conducting tissues on the inner heart surfaces have also been developed and are also sometimes used. In the past few decades, pacemakers and other implantable electrical devices that stimulate the heart have emerged and are being implanted in ever-growing numbers.

One of the catheter-based procedures is ablation. Little bits

---

15   https://www.fda.gov/RegulatoryInformation/Guidances/ucm404975.htm#
description

of tissue on the inner surface of the heart walls are injured (or ablated) to interfere with abnormal generation or conduction of the heart's own electrical impulses.

Ablation can also be done at the time of open-heart surgery if the patient has associated structural problems that require correction.

One of my close friends and colleagues in Groningen developed tachycardia similar to mine. He had a catheter ablation procedure, where eight or nine lesions were made in one of the internal heart walls. Each of these ablations was about 4 mm deep and perhaps 8 or 10 mm in diameter. Though my friend was initially quite happy with the results, the positive effects disappeared after a few weeks and a second round of ablations was required. Time will tell how all this works out for my friend.

. . .

These essays make two important points. First, Bernie needed to gain some control of his problems. He did it through intellectualizing, writing about the technology of arrhythmia management. Second, after all this science, he engages in the absolutely typical human reaction of reporting an individual case. Bernie wrote about his friend's ablation procedure.

There is almost nothing appropriate that a doctor can say in response to the patient who gives an anecdotal report about a friend, relative, or neighbor who underwent a recommended procedure "and it didn't work." It's hard to believe that a trained scientist like Bernie would do this here.

In response to the anecdote, I'm often tempted to say, "Well, it works most of the time."

Most people don't seem to find that accurate information very reassuring.

I will also freely admit to my urge to offer this observation: "Maybe the doctor who performed the procedure was just a klutz."

Such a comment carries a very real risk of a visit from a representative of the state medical board, a lawyer, or both.

I have often wished that I had time in an office visit to sit down and ask, "What are you really trying to tell me with this story?"

Patience remains a virtue, particularly in this era of rushed schedules.

CHAPTER 7

A Brief Aside

Everyone who knew Bernie heard him think out loud about bicycle riders in the Tour de France. It was one of his favorite subjects, and every time I heard him tell this tale, I enjoyed it.

. . .

About five liters of blood leave a resting heart every minute. As more oxygen and fuel are needed, heart rate and blood flow increase. Blood is directed to the organs or muscles where it is needed; thus, exercising and well-trained cyclists have around 85 to 90 percent of the blood pumped each minute going to their legs. These people have prodigious power outputs. They can generate as high as 2,500 watts—ten times more than what I can do—for a few minutes on the cycle used for stress testing.

The power output of long distance cyclists makes for an interesting story. There are a number of famous European long-distance races, such as the Tour de France and Giro d'Italia (the Italian tour). These races cover several thousand kilometers during ten to fifteen days of cycling. Daily Tour de France stages vary in distance from 200 to 300 km (120 to 180 miles), and each stage may include two or three climbs of 1,000 to 1,500 meters each. Racing cyclists maintain average speeds of 40 to 45 km per hour (about 25 mph).

Like any other engine, cyclists need fuel. These racers require as much as nine-thousand calories per day. If we go back to a little basic chemistry, a Tour cyclist must take in 2 kg (or about 4.4 lb.) of glucose (sugar) just to power his bicycle and a little more to keep his body in good condition. Now, how does this rider consume 2 kg of glucose or similar energy-containing molecules?

How about eating potatoes? Potatoes contain starch, which is essentially only glucose. Neglecting some minor adjustments, the required 2 kg glucose is the equivalent of about 11 kg (22 lb.) of potatoes, because the potatoes are about 80 percent water.

Pasta contains no water, so it is better fuel than potatoes. But because pasta is cooked in water and absorbs some of that liquid, a cyclist must consume about 3 kg (6.5 lb.) of pasta.

Sucrose or high-fructose drinks are another option. Most contain 10 to 12 percent sugar or high fructose, or 100 to 120 g of sugar per liter, so our cyclist would have to drink sixteen to twenty liters (four to five gallons) to take in the needed 2 kg of glucose.

Professional cyclists riding in the Tour are generally small to medium sized and definitely not overweight. At the start of the day's stage, they cannot take in all this fuel in one sitting. This intake has to be properly managed by trainers and cyclists to ensure a sufficient energy supply and avoid breaking down some of the riders' protein body mass.

Victory comes to those who are in top shape and have most of these parameters under control. Lance Armstrong survived cancer and won the Tour de France seven times. Performance-enhancing drugs may have helped a little. Still, in the end, the heart must pump the blood around; the glucose or fats must be transported to muscle tissue, and the fuel must be converted into mechanical work.

I once made a back-of-the-envelope calculation. It showed that four racing cyclists have to burn more calories than a Renault car—rolling along at the same speed and carrying the same four people—would burn.

This makes sense, because that single little car experiences less wind resistance than do the four cyclists, even if they ride in close formation.

What I love about all these things is that so much of what we encounter, from the plants and animals we eat to the Apollo rockets that carried a few of us to the moon, is connected, and just a few little numbers will often suffice to show the connection among all of it.

· · ·

I cannot read the last two paragraphs without smiling. The Renault calculation summarizes his worldview. As Bernie would say "what I love," those eyebrows would start to rise and the Witholt smile would form.

Bernie admired Lance Armstrong and was sorely disappointed when the doping scandals surfaced. His comment that "drugs may have helped a little" was an indirect way of coming to terms with the issue. In his view, despite the controversies, Armstrong remained a physiological marvel.

As Bernie saw it, doping and performance-enhancing drugs could have added only a small increment to Armstrong's overall performance. That increment may have contributed to his wearing the yellow jersey, but completing the Tour seven times was simply a remarkable feat.

As usual, it's hard to argue with his logic.

CHAPTER 8

Taking the Challenge of Rowing a Bit Too Far

Sometimes an experiment goes wrong. Here, Bernie pushed too far, and he acknowledged his fear of the outcome—but only by reporting his methods in detail and working up to it.

• • •

I bought an ergometer, the Concept2 Indoor Rower, in mid-2003 (the version with a Polar belt and capability to track heart rate and power output with each stroke).

The Polar heart rate monitor consisted of a chest band with two electrodes that sensed the electrical activity of the heart, just like the electrodes your doctor or nurse attaches to the chest and abdomen to record an electrocardiogram.

The monitor transmits electrical signals from the heart to a little receiver that calculates the heart rate. The receiver I used was built into a wristwatch, which showed the heart rate as a number of beats per minute. The same kind of receiver can also be built into other devices, such as the small bike-mounted computers cyclists use to follow their heart rates, their distance traveled, the rate at which they crank the pedals, the power developed by the left and right legs at each turn of the pedals, and additional information about the temperature, the elevation of the terrain, and other information. Collecting more and more data is possible as new sensors are developed.

Back to the simple heart rate monitor.

I'm especially interested in how my heart behaves when I row in a boat, and for that I use the wristwatch monitor. If I row on my rowing machine, I can use the fixed monitor attached to the machine.

• • •

This type of monitoring is pretty straightforward to anyone who owns a Fitbit. But Bernie is about to go into detail about his experimental methods. The important point is that he is going to subject himself to some rather dangerous "clinical research."

• • •

Newer monitors store heart rates and the time at which each new rate was measured. I can transfer that data into a computer to produce various graphs. A graph of heart rate versus time is interesting. It shows the heart rate changing as one begins to run, cycle, row, whatever one wants to do. It can show the effects of slowly and steadily walking on the level, going up a gentle incline, taking some stairs, and then walking on a level street for a while.

An illness might reduce performance. Your heart rate, for example, is 10 bpm higher (135 instead of 125 bpm) at the top of a hill you walk up several times per week. As you recover, your heart rate might come back to what you are used to seeing.

. . .

If you decide to improve your walking or hiking performance by training, you might notice your heart rate decreases by five or ten beats on a particular stretch. I find these changes very satisfying, especially if the pattern is a nice, regular, and clear decrease in heart rate over a period of several months.

The Concept2 is a rowing machine that closely simulates the movements and effort required to row a racing shell on water. When sitting in a boat such as a single or double scull, rowers place two oars in the water and pull on them to lever the boat forward. On the rowing machine, the rower pulls on a double handle attached to a chain. The chain turns a wheel equipped with air scoops; the faster the rower pulls, the more power is needed to overcome the air resistance of the rotating scoops.

The rowing machine, or ergometer, has a monitor that records and displays all of the relevant parameters: power developed at each pull of the chain, or "stroke"; the rate at which the handles are pulled; strokes per minute; the "distance" traveled per stroke; amount of time needed to "row" a distance; and the rower's heart rate during the entire process. The machine can be set to record data for a fixed distance or time and to repeat a series of exercises followed by preset rest times.

University, club, and national teams all use ergometers not only to train for strength and endurance but also to measure individual performance. Coaches use recorded data to select and match rowers, thus making successful crews for eights, fours, and even pairs or doubles. In fact, ergometers have been perfected to such an extent that they can be used for races in their own right.

I bought the rowing machine to supplement my efforts with exercises and walking to get my body back into acceptable condition. I also thought it would be useful to be able to record various measures of effort versus heart rate—to learn a little more about what did (and what did not) affect my heart rates.

Most of my rowing experience was on water. While in college, I rowed for four years on the Connecticut River and on Philadelphia's Schuylkill River with Roger, one of my college classmates. Later, I rowed with a club in Groningen that included all sorts of more or less experienced oarsmen. My last major competitions dated back to 1992 in Zurich when I first arrived there. I had not had time for on-the-water rowing since then. Still, I thought it a fantastic sport.

A decade after my last experience on the water, I set up the ergometer in my basement. I watched my heart rate as I tried out a few things—gently rowing some modest stretches of a few kilometers at a low stroke rate. I saw the same kind of heart rate instability I'd seen when I had tried running a few years earlier. I set up my computer to record and show the data using a program provided with the Concept2; now I could see heart rate patterns on the display, and I could save them for future reference.

• • •

So far, so good, Bernie. But you are doing this all alone on your Concept2, without any observation or supervision, right?

• • •

One day, I had a rather strange experience. After I had rowed 3 or 4 km at a modest pace, I suddenly felt as though I were no longer sitting on the rowing machine. I felt I had floated off into a space, far above the machine, higher than the ceiling would have allowed. I don't remember seeing my heart rate on the display. In fact, I did not then—nor do I now—remember how exactly I experienced coming back down. At some point, I was once again sitting on the machine, and I felt rather shaken. What had happened? Did I pass out? I did not have a tachycardia. Or, at least, my ICD had done nothing.

I was scared. Was I going too far with this presumably rational approach? My first instinct was to head to the hospital and contact my heart rhythm specialist. What, however, would he be able to do? I would once again be subjected to the usual routine: an ECG, a few blood samples, a suggestion to have an MRI or a CAT scan, whatever. Maybe I would even be told to take a new pill. I went back upstairs and did not return to rowing for a few weeks.

When I finally did return and resumed my exercises, I experienced a gradual improvement in fitness. I never again experienced that floating sensation.

· · ·

Bernie's usual rhythm disturbances were what cardiologists call monomorphic ventricular tachycardia. When he had a tachycardia, his heart rate during the arrhythmia was a stable 240 bpm on every recorded occasion. This rate is too fast for the heart to fill properly, but if Bernie would sit or lie down during an episode, he would not lose consciousness.

In the previously described event, Bernie carefully set up his exercise and monitoring equipment, which then provoked what was almost certainly a very different problem. Though there is no way to know, his description of the event suggests an episode of ventricular fibrillation (VF) that spontaneously terminated. Self-terminating VF is rare. Older cardiologists (and I qualify for this category) sometimes used to see it induced by an antihistamine drug that is no longer on the market.

If my suspicion is correct, what my friend experienced was truly a near-death experience. He probably had a severe reduction of blood flow to the brain for a short time, like an aerobatic pilot pulling too many Gs.

Bernie was seldom frightened, but this time, he had every reason to be. In his own way, he was pushing the envelope.

CHAPTER 9

Exercise Reduces the Need for Sleep

This short musing from Bernie gives another typical example of his mind at work. I don't know how he envisioned it fitting into his narrative. I've included it at this point to demonstrate how the restless self-awareness, self-experimentation, and quantification described in Bernie's experiments on the ergometer extended to every facet of his life.

. . .

I have often noticed that exercise reduces my need to sleep. One hour of exercise seems to be equivalent to about half or three-quarters of an hour of sleep. What is the connection here?

. . .

What did he just say? "Exercise reduces my need to sleep"—now, that's interesting! Anyone else I know would have turned that sentence around to say, "I sleep better after I exercise a bit." And they would leave it at that.

. . .

We relax during sleep. Similar to Holter heart rate monitoring, my blood pressure was recently monitored for a twenty-four-hour period. My blood pressure fell from an average of 130/80 during the day to 100/60 at night. Evidently all or most muscles relaxed to the point that blood flow was almost unimpeded.

Almost all exercise entails a continuous cycle of effort and relaxation. Isometrics, a popular form of exercise some twenty or thirty years ago, might have required longer stretches of continuous pressure on certain muscles. Even with isometrics' particular and sustained muscle contractions, every effort was followed by an interval of relaxation.

The intermittent periods of relaxation during exercise may, in some way, be similar to the relaxation experienced while sleeping. Intensive effort is clearly accompanied by higher blood pressure, so it is not unreasonable to suppose that relaxation between efforts would or could result in lowered blood pressure.

. . .

Watch, and you can see Bernie's hypothesis starting to form. As soon as Bernie gets to a statement beginning with "if," a "then" statement is sure to follow.

. . .

If these periods do indeed compensate for some of the relaxation time experienced during sleep, then it would appear that normal waking time (whether active or inactive) produces less relaxation as does exercise, with its intermittent effort and relaxation.

So, this suggests that a day with *some* exercise is more relaxing than a day with *no specific effort.* This is not entirely obvious; it might appear that engaging in daily exercise (fifteen minutes, thirty minutes, an hour) would require more overall effort than not doing so. In any case, it might well be that a little effort every day is more relaxing than no effort at all.

This takes us to Compound X, a villainous and as yet unidentified substance that contributes to my heart problems.[16] Let's suppose that a little bit of exercise—perhaps exercise that affects all rather than just a few muscles—eliminates any Compound X that has accumulated during the day. If that's so, then there might be several effects to note when comparing to situations when there is no daily exercise:

- lower blood pressure
- reduced work done by the heart to pump blood
- fewer likely episodes of tachycardia
- overall, a more relaxed entire system

Those results seem rather obvious, since they are part of our daily experience. The list's only uncommon item refers to tachycardia. In this scenario, these can be viewed as symptoms of a body less than desirably balanced. I can be off-balance for a long time, and sooner or later, tachycardia will occur.

I can treat the symptom. However, it is better to understand and resolve the source of the symptom. If the previous is correct (or perhaps only partially correct), then it is best to follow the advice I have received all my life from all these well-meaning people, starting with my parents and teachers and later, my wife

---

16   Bernie invented "Compound X," a hypothetical compound made by his body.

and aging friends who are all gradually facing the same battles as we grow older.

It would of course still be nice to identify Compound X and see how it does whatever it does.

• • •

This is a nice example of Bernie taking something pretty straightforward and tying it into a real intellectual knot. He tries to link his observation of his heart problems with the hypothetical Compound X, "a villainous and as yet unidentified substance" that disrupts his normal heart rhythm from time to time. You can almost see the masked Compound X in a black cloak, skulking in the background and accumulating henchmen in the absence of exercise. The idea is about as sound as phlogiston or miasma. After thinking it through, Bernie backs off for a second, shrugs, and thinks that perhaps he should follow the advice of his family and friends.

Then, the eyebrows lift, the eyes sparkle, the smile breaks out, and Bernie's back on the trail of Compound X.

The scientist can deal with his symptoms, but the patient yearns for hand-to-hand combat with their villainous source.

Before going any further, let me point out that the ideas Bernie expressed here deviate widely from accepted concepts of the physiology of rest, exercise, and blood supply autoregulation. Since bacteria don't have circulatory systems, none of this really mattered to him.

CHAPTER 10

On the Water Again
(2004–2005)

By 2004, Bernie had dealt with his arrhythmia for five years. In his telling, he seems to have more or less made peace with it. During the 2004–2005 period, he and his heart got along quite well. He had learned to gradually increase and decrease his heart rate by carefully controlling the intensity of his activity.

This process of constantly monitoring and slowly adjusting his heart rate during his training activity helped him to avoid conditions that made him physiologically vulnerable to triggering an onset of tachycardia. He even achieved a high level of fitness.

In addition, Bernie's ability to exercise vigorously after carefully warming up suggests that his heart's pumping function had remained nearly intact.

• • •

Seven or eight of the major German technical universities had a yearly rowing regatta in which teams of professors competed for what was known as the "Professoren Achter Cup."[17] Sometime in early 2004, we ETH Zurich professors received a letter from our rector, telling us that the German universities wished to expand the competition by including crews from ETH Zurich and University of Vienna. The rector wished to know who might be interested in participating.

ETH Zurich would supply a coach and fly the crew to Munich, where the competition was to be held in the Olympic basin.[18]

I reread the letter a few times. This was exciting, really exciting. And crazy, of course.

Here I was, sixty-three years old, in a most uncertain state and shape, thinking I could train to compete for a place rowing in an eight against any number of my three hundred colleagues.[19] And who knew at what risk? And then, if this worked out, row several heats against eight or nine other boats?

Why not though? I might as well find out what was still possible.

I was one of twenty who signed up, and I checked them all out. How old were they? Did they have experience? They were all younger; some were still in their late thirties. Some looked very capable; they were skiers, runners, and bikers.

So it was that I started rowing on water again in May 2004, an aspiring member of ETH Zurich's "Professoren Achter" crew,

---

17   The "Professoren Achter Cup" was an informal event, not a sanctioned competition.

18   The rowing course, built for the 1972 Olympic games, is just outside Munich.

19   An "eight" actually consists of nine crew members: eight rowers (four with a single oar reaching out on the starboard side of the shell and four with a single oar reaching out on the port side) and a coxswain, who coordinates all of the boat's activities and steers the shell by operating the rudder, which is pulled toward one side or the other via two lines.

invited to compete in Munich against most of the German technical universities.

In 2004, ETH Zurich did not have many female professors (maybe eight or ten), but one colleague, Sarah Springman, did sign up. In the past, Sarah had competed in twelve triathlons, typically finishing among the top ten women in Europe. Five of those twelve triathlon events were the Ironman World Championship in Hawaii. She'd switched to rowing when triathlon training began to interfere with her academic work.

I later learned that when Sarah was in her twenties, she had gotten four other women to join her in a race that entailed biking 50 or 60 km from London to Reading, then swimming in relay to Le Havre, France, with every participant spending at least one hour in the North Sea (which, in mid-October, was already down to 12°C/54°F), before finally biking or running in relay to Paris. Her competition included a team from the US Navy SEALs and a similar group from the US Army. Though the women were slower than these men on the roads, they outlasted them in the water; both the SEALs and the Army group were disqualified because not all of them had spent at least one hour in the North Sea.

I also spent time rowing with various other people in small boats, with a nice outing in early May with the *breitensportler* of the Grasshopper rowing club. We rowed in England, going from Oxford to Henley in three 25–30 km (15–18 miles) stretches. Good fun, lots of beer, and good food along the way. My wife, Renske, was there part of the time, spending the rest of it with our friends Franzie and Brigitte in London.

Our coach, Florian, was a graduate student who was working on a PhD in inorganic chemistry. He was also a rowing machine enthusiast who operated a clinic with forty or fifty ergometers in one of ETH Zurich's larger gyms. We trained twice a week at six a.m. when there was no traffic on Lake Zurich. The Alps at one end of the lake seemed to practically fall in the water, though they were at least thirty or forty kilometers to the east. Just wonderful.

During this same period, I met Markus Wyss, the new husband of one of our Zurich friends. As it turned out, Markus was much interested in picking up rowing again. We determined we both liked rowing a double scull. The double is a fast racing shell with two oarsmen, each rowing with one scull. "Scull" is a smaller oar pulled with one hand; the larger oar, or "sweep," requires an oarsman to pull with both hands. Thus, an oarsman in a scull uses two oars; in a sweep, only one.[20]

We decided to try a double scull at a small rowing club. We also took out memberships at a larger club, where the ETH Zurich professor's eight was housed.

The result of all this was that, after several years of near total inactivity, I was suddenly rowing four or five times per week, always at six a.m., with some additional work on my Concept2 ergometer, which enabled me to track my heart's performance.

It was all rather ridiculous and at the same time totally exciting. Markus, my new rowing mate, at 2.06 m (6'9") was 20 cm (8") taller than I; at 106 kg (234 lb.), he was also 20 kg (44 lb.) heavier. And he was twenty years younger. A former member of the Swiss National eight, Markus had me working hard to keep the double properly moving. My fellow professors and our young coach ensured another two good mornings every week.

---

20   Sculls are usually single (one oarsman) or double (two). Quad sculls (four) are rare. Sculls do not have coxswains to steer. Sweeps are pairs, fours, or eights; fours and eights have a coxswain who faces forward and steers.

Early in July, eight of us and Florian, our coach, made our way to Munich, rigged up a boat, had a good dinner with a glass of wine, which I found slightly shocking (these, however, were new times).

During our first practice start, Florian raised his eyes to the heavens, imploring for clemency and assorted blessings. It was a disaster, I suppose. But professors have mental resources. Later that day, we won our first heat by beating Dresden. Then, we won the second, beating Darmstadt. In the final, against the Technical University of Aachen, the judges declared us the winners in a photo finish.

It was all quite exciting, with a fine dinner and speeches. But most wonderful was having been part of this.

When I went to my heart rhythm specialist for my half yearly ICD check, he looked at the data and asked, "What did you do on July 7? I see three sequences ending at 170 bpm . . . "

I responded: "Ah, yes. Those were the finishes of three heats against the German technical universities."

It all fit. All this enabled by four years of 100 mg per day of flecainide. Thanks to the organic chemists who first produced it and those clinicians who first tested it. I should find out who they are. Or were.

I could not help mailing a happy note to Roger, my rowing friend at Amherst and double scull teammate in Philadelphia during the summer of 1963 at the Vesper Boat Club.

• • •

Bernie shares an important insight in the paragraphs above. He and his teammates had just won a significant race, and he tells us, " . . . most wonderful was having been part of this."

The camaraderie, the sense of acceptance as one of the team—those were the good parts. And with Bernie, a team's bonds lasted. As he says, "I could not help mailing a happy note to Roger . . . my double scull teammate." He knew that I would share his joy in the moment, and I did.

CHAPTER 11

Symptoms Again:
Tachycardia in Groningen

My ICD was routinely replaced in April 2005 to provide a fresh battery.

• • •

The replacement procedure for pacemakers or ICDs is now a one-day or even an outpatient procedure. The device sits in a pocket under the skin. After routine sterile preparations, the cardiologist administers local anesthesia, opens the pocket, and uses a sterile Allen wrench to loosen the device's electrode connections. Then the cardiologist slides the ICD or pacemaker off the wires and slides on a new one. All that's left is to tighten the connections and close the pocket.

• • •

This year, the rector did not ask us to put together an ETH Zurich "Professoren Achter" team. Most of my younger colleagues were deeply immersed in their work. I was less so, and we had promised our German rowing friends we would repeat that

2004 competition in Zurich the following year. So, we invited the University of Zurich to join us in hosting a regatta for the same group of German technical universities. In addition, we invited Delft and Imperial College (the Dutch and British technical universities) to come row in Zurich, too.

Florian came back to coach us again, and once again, we won. That year, 2005, was my best year rowing since 1998 (or perhaps even earlier). I looked forward to further improvements in 2006, but as I have learned since then, there are limits.

Despite all of the training and rowing, I still had an occasional tachycardia, usually associated with the fact that I did not feel all that well, was perhaps short on blood sugar, or ran into a bit of stress.

On one such occasion, I was in Groningen to give a lecture for an afternoon symposium on high-tech start-up creation at universities. I was staying with my old friends Otto and Susan, and we walked over to the Academy building; it was just a short walk, but I could feel I needed some juice. When we arrived in the old Senate room, there was no juice, and the video installation had been improperly set up. Otto disappeared to talk to various guests, and I stood around, fussing with the projector, which left no time to get the juice I clearly needed.

I was the second speaker. As I stood there speaking and using my laptop and mouse to go through a set of slides, I grew increasingly irritated with one of my old colleagues. One of my good friends in the chemistry department, he had retired around 1988 when I chaired the department. Then, he stayed on to develop a company that he set up with the help of the science park organization that we had created five years earlier. He had been quite successful, building the company into a profitable and effective

100- to 120-employee organic chemistry research organization. Now this respectable octogenarian-plus was sitting in the first row, giving a continuous commentary while I spoke.

• • •

Bernie's daily adaptations to his heart disease involved a large measure of denial. He must have felt some anxiety about this invited lecture. After all, he faced a group of colleagues who would be scientifically critical. The projector malfunction irritated him. His old colleague in the first row certainly managed to get under his skin. Was he more upset than he knew?

• • •

As I talked, he kept grumbling along. Suddenly, Otto, who was sitting in the back of the room, stood up. I felt an electrical shock of some sort, but I was totally focused on my talk and my old colleague's annoying commentary. I wondered what had happened. It seemed as though I had felt a shock from the mouse. From the mouse; how could that be?

Otto was still standing, looking concerned. The people in the first few rows looked a bit nonplussed. I then realized my ICD had done its job.

I leaned into the lectern. I asked for some juice, waited one or two minutes, and then resumed my talk. I explained to the audience that they had just witnessed an application of high tech in the medical sector, an ICD functioning. There was relief all around; Otto sat down, and my old friend said nothing more for the rest of the talk.

I learned two lessons.

First: Get some juice when you feel you need it.

Second: A good friend sitting some fifteen meters (fifty feet) or so away could detect a tachycardia onset. (That was interesting. Otto is a very good friend. Others might see less.)

• • •

There was, of course, a third lesson, one that Bernie did not like to discuss: the role that emotional stress played in triggering some of his tachycardias. At the Zurich Stock Exchange, he was irritated that none of his younger colleagues offered him a seat. Similarly, the irritating continuous comments from his older colleague helped set the stage for this episode in Groningen. He never seemed to have much interest in the relationship of his emotional state to his tachycardia.

Whatever internal signals he sensed as "needing some juice" probably were something much more biologically complex than simply "low blood sugar." In this story, he must have been under considerable emotional stress in his role as an invited speaker and from his elderly colleague's uninvited commentary. Both hypoglycemia (low blood sugar) and stress arousal (fight or flight situations) trigger a surge of rapid activation of the sympathetic nervous system. Physiologically, the responses are similar to an abrupt transition from rest to exercise. The circumstances provided the physiologic stimuli that he knew would make him vulnerable to tachycardia.

In any event, we get a sense of how completely focused he was on the task at hand from the fact that, at first, he thought the ICD shock had come from the computer mouse in his hand. Many patients have described their ICD shocks for me, and no one else has ever thought the sensation came from a computer mouse. Most patients find it VERY unpleasant.

CHAPTER 12

Retirement: Bernie Joins the Medical Establishment

I retired at the end of March 2006.

• • •

The mandatory retirement age in Switzerland for men is sixty-five. There was no choice.

• • •

My successors, led by Professor Ruedi Aebersold from the Institute for Systems Biology in Seattle, created the Institute of Molecular Systems Biology to succeed ETH Zurich's Institute of Biotechnology. Other newly nominated professors joined Ruedi, and soon the institute was an active beehive once again. Ruedi offered me an office and a lab. I accepted and spent a year cleaning up the administrative leftovers of my old institute and watching my last few doctoral students finish their work.

Later that year, I was asked to join the Supervisory Board of the University Medical Center Groningen (UMCG) in the

Netherlands. The Medical Center included the former University Medical School and the Academic Hospital in Groningen. All the Dutch universities had initiated the process of combining medical schools with academic hospitals a few years earlier. By 2005, there were eight academic medical centers in the Netherlands: two in Amsterdam and one each in the major Dutch universities elsewhere (Rotterdam, Leiden, Utrecht, Nijmegen, Maastricht, and Groningen).

Each of these centers took in about four hundred first-year medical students, along with some centers' additional dental and physical education students. Each hospital had 1,200 to 1,500 beds and a budget of around €1 billion per year. Funding came from a combination of medical insurance companies, government agencies, research grants, and patients' modest payments for private medical services.

UMCG's Supervisory Board consisted of five members who had various areas of expertise. The board's two major roles were to appoint the executive management, including the dean of the medical school, and approve the yearly budget. We met with the medical center management five or six times a year to deal with these and various other matters. For example, we dealt with patient satisfaction or medical practice concerns that cropped up now and then. These areas would become progressively more important over the ensuing years.

• • •

Typically modest Bernie. UMCG was a major Dutch medical center. As a young scientist, Groningen had been his first academic appointment, and he was delighted to return as a member of the institution's Supervisory Board.

...

Not long after I joined the board, I decided to participate in a set of internal audits. Typically, an audit team included several members of one hospital unit: a medical specialist, physician or researcher, senior nurse, and possibly an administrator. This team visited and did an audit of another hospital unit that was also represented by several staff members. The audits often involved specialized hospital areas, such as the newborn intensive care unit or the surgery theatres; audits might also cover special functions, procedures, and protocols (such as information technology infrastructure, relations between nursing and medical staff, the handling of medications, and so on).

I spent a week in Groningen, participating in four of the ten scheduled audits. The reality, not unexpectedly, was a little less perfect than the plan. Nursing staff had difficulty dealing with the attitudes of the medical staff; there were issues about equipment.

In short, we saw the daily operational problems that arise in all medical institutions. On the other hand, most of the people I saw and listened to were caring and devoted to their jobs. Everyone was impressive. They were, of course, only a small sample of UMCG's ten thousand employees.

At one point I chatted with the heart rhythm specialists. Similar to the University Hospital in Zurich, amiodarone was their first choice of medication for ventricular tachycardia. Problematic, but what else is there? The UMCG specialists implanted three hundred ICDs per year.

Finances are always a concern at any medical center. I thought that I understood the financial structure of the Dutch universities and various funding agencies well enough. After all, during my years at the University of Groningen I had, at one time or another, sat on most of the relevant faculty and university committees. I had been the chemistry department's chairman for years, started several research centers, and looked for funding wherever available. After I moved to Zurich, I was asked to join the scientific advisory boards of several of the large German biotechnology institutes; again, funding often came up. In the Netherlands, I had sat on many of the national committees that distributed funding for large inter-university and academic-industrial projects in all areas of science.

So, with all this experience, I believed that these areas of Dutch research priorities, university budgets, funding sources, department finances, personnel matters, and research money, held few secrets for me. Not so, as I found out when I joined the UMCG Supervisory Board.

Not long ago I heard a lecture about how the US finances health and medicine by a professor who held appointments in both economics and medicine at Stanford. At one point, he was asked whether the US might learn something about financing health care and medical costs from other countries. "Yes," he answered. "Two come to mind: the Netherlands and Switzerland." He then proceeded to discuss the financial approaches these countries use. I found this interesting, since I have experienced these two health care systems firsthand for the past forty years.

Essentially, these two countries have no private universities. All universities are funded almost entirely by the state. In the Netherlands, funding occurs at the national level and, with the exception of the two technical universities (ETH Zurich and Ecole Ploytechnique Federale de Lausanne, or EPFL, one of the Swiss Federal Insitutes of Technology), by the cantons in Switzerland. Research and teaching are outstanding in both countries.

There is, of course, always jostling about who is best in physics, chemistry, molecular biology, immunology, neurosciences, and so on, but every university has stars in several areas, and no mediocre universities exist anywhere in these two countries. Some of the funding for research and special teaching programs comes from national and EU funding bodies. Industrial money plays a modest role, but the bulk of the funding for both Dutch and Swiss universities comes directly from the national and provincial governments, much like the funding of state universities in the US.

Students pay some tuition; this has increased from ten or twenty years ago, although it remains quite modest compared to total university budgets and costs per student. Still, at €2,000 to CHF 3,000 (Swiss francs) per year, student tuition fees are a pittance compared to costs in the US at comparable schools.

In the Netherlands and Switzerland, students can easily obtain grants and loans to cover their cost of living, although more students live at home in the latter country. As an aside, professional schools in both countries accommodate at least as many students in the same age range as do universities. Professional schools typically educate engineers, technical personnel, and teachers, while universities educate lawyers, physicians, and natural and social scientists.

The medical schools are an integral part of these European universities. The academic hospitals are not; on one hand, they operate at the interface of patient services and on the other, they perform teaching, research, and public service. This is important to the income of the academic hospitals; the bulk of their funding comes from patient care, either directly or via medical insurers.

Focusing on the Netherlands, I was surprised to learn that the Dutch system was based on bulk arrangements between insurers and health providers rather than billing individual patients for specific services, with insurers then reimbursing the patients for all or part of the cost. Insurers and individual hospitals or hospital groups agree on the amount of the insurer's total payment for a given year based on projected medical services to be delivered: The cost of so many hip replacements, appendix removals, cataract treatments, and on and on, is based on previous experience, actuarial data, and various negotiations.

Dutch hospitals then admit patients, calculating their total costs of treatment on a series of standard menu items (hours in surgery, days in a bed, meals, medication, specialists, nursing staff, etc.) and compensating each of the units involved in the patients' treatment. Additional income streams come from the national Department of Health, charitable foundations, and special funds from various sources for large research programs.

Amazingly, income and costs have been in balance most of the time.

In addition to the routine patient services, there is spending for new buildings, new facilities and equipment, and new programs; sometimes, there is even a modest profit (but never more than a fraction of 1 percent).

All of this made sense to me. After a few years on the Supervisory Board of UMCG's Medical Center, I believed I understood what was happening, as far as finances were concerned.

Then, more details surfaced while I was traveling by train to Amsterdam with two of my fellow supervisors. One was a professor in the medical school of the Free University of Amsterdam, and the other was the former minister of environmental affairs, former governor of the province of Groningen, and a consultant who was deeply involved in the negotiations between medical insurers and the Dutch government,

These two supervisors informed me that all of the Dutch medical insurers were branches of just four large insurers. The ostensible competition between insurers affected only about 5 percent of the total Dutch health care market. The government determined health care costs and then made a commitment to voters; at the end of each year, the Dutch Department of Health evaluated contracts between insurers and those academic and other hospitals. If total health costs exceeded that government-determined amount, the commitment to voters was honored. If they did not, hospitals were instructed to reimburse the excess to the insurers, who in turn, adjusted their premiums accordingly.

All of this, my friends explained, was necessary to ensure that the Netherlands' average health costs remained in line with earlier projections, which was important to guarantee Dutch citizens (or perhaps better yet, Dutch *voters*) a certain amount of disposable income.

I, a reasonably sophisticated academic, lived in the Netherlands from 1972 to 1992. This explanation of health care funding was, however, news to me ... and very interesting news. When I first moved from the University of California to the University of Groningen, I had had my doubts about a number of Dutch social institutions, particularly those meant to protect people less able to protect themselves. These social institutions included subsidies for renters with low incomes and reduced medical insurance rates for those who could not afford good medical care. The Netherlands had a variety of compensatory mechanisms to eliminate the effects of lower incomes. As I came to understand the system better, I began to see its charms. The system was not about blocking those who want to conquer the world and be paid accordingly. It was about protecting those who do not want, or are unable, to join that particular game.

It's OK. The Dutch simply do not worry all that much about their income. The basics are there for everybody (as is much more that is not all that basic). Every young person can go to a professional school or university, depending a little—but only a little—on past school performance. Those who lose their jobs receive various assistance. There is nothing shameful about this in the Netherlands. In Switzerland, job loss is viewed a little differently, but then Swiss unemployment is usually between 3 and 5 percent.

So, after all these years, I discovered little old Holland prefers a capitalist system, though one that does not like to take chances with really important matters (health being one of them). Very interesting. And that's OK, now that I have thought about it for a while.

· · ·

The founder of several biotech firms, Bernie was an entrepreneur. Unlike some of his American counterparts, he freely accepted those who marched to different drummers: "As I understood the system better, I began to see its charms. It was not about blocking those who want to conquer the world and be paid accordingly. It was about protecting those who do not want, or are unable, to join this particular game."

He meant "charms"; he chose the word carefully. He wanted to work hard, and he did. But he did not look down on those who didn't or couldn't.

By the way, did you notice, a few pages back, the paragraph about chatting with the electrophysiologists at UMGC? They implanted three hundred ICDs per year! He just dropped that statistic in there, like saying, "And on Tuesday, it rained." He's minimizing the conversation. He wanted to talk to the Groningen specialists, but he didn't want to report the details.

This is another patient strategy that clinicians learn to recognize over the years. The response, of course, should be, "Tell me more about that . . . "

CHAPTER 13

UMCG: Patients as Customers

Patients rarely have the opportunity to see the medical world from the administrative side. Bernie, however, fully engaged with his role as a member of the medical center's board. He had the ability to focus on his supervisory role, but Bernie brought along the experience of having been a patient.

• • •

Before 2007, I knew that hospitals were complex organizations—more complex than the faculties of a university and more complex than most other industrial and commercial organizations. As I saw it, their major task was to take in sick people and send them home, if not healthy, at least in better shape than when they arrived. All other hospital activities served this goal, either directly or indirectly. This applies to research, which supports future clinical work (or at least tries to do so).

Somehow, I expected the same goal to be shared among the people working in hospitals—nurses, doctors, specialists—and general physicians in private practices. This may sound naïve, but the premeds and medical students I knew back in the 1960s often claimed (and undoubtedly believed) they were going to serve mankind. Following medical school, they took the Hippocratic

Oath, and I do not recall anyone being cynical about that. This is probably still true. I believe that, at their core, today's young people are not all that different from young people fifty years ago. I have never met a student who does not want to do something useful, exciting, and interesting. They want a future. They sometimes worry. Sometimes, they need a little help.

Some things,though, have changed or are different from what I expected them to still be. Students adopt available role models, but those role models are not always as good as they might be.

Large hospitals have to be run like businesses, and inevitably, they adopt habits that serve the business. Costs must be covered. New techniques must be viable. We may need to introduce these approaches because other large hospitals are making similar investments. Those new approaches with their large investments will require sufficient numbers of patients. Patients have become customers, and we cannot risk losing customers to our competitors.

Concerns for Patients

As our academic hospitals morph into more commercial organizations, the patient base begins to look more like a market with distinct groups of customers. In the Netherlands, there exist nationwide patient organizations. Some are formal, legally established entities; others are informal. Both have a variety of roles meant to ensure that patient interests are taken seriously.

In addition to these patient groups, there is a national Health Care Inspectorate (the Inspectie voor Gezondheidszorg, or IGZ), which reviews medical accidents and incidents at all hospitals, public and private. Hospitals report any accidents or incidents considered sufficiently serious; patients or patient groups can also bring adverse events to the attention of the IGZ. In addition, the IGZ pays yearly visits to all hospitals and carries out general inspections, followed by advice, instructions, and, when necessary, sanctions. The results of its inspections are evaluated and may result in new instructions and sanctions.

...

When you think about it, the corporate model of medical care has to include quality-control functions. This trend began in the US in the 1970s as hospitals faced more stringent Medicare requirements. Until quite recently, most quality-control measures in US health care, however, were at the local level.

...

This Dutch bureaucratic system works slowly; cases may be dealt with over periods of one to three years. Sometimes, when patients feel that they have been badly treated or ignored by the system, either by the hospitals or by the IGZ, they may avail themselves of the National Ombudsman of the Netherlands. In addition, the media, which has become quite interested in affairs of the medical care sector, often helps these patients gain attention.

The National Ombudsman is much more than a single office holder who deals with registered complaints. Its staff of 170 specifically addresses public concerns and individual citizen complaints that relate to malfunctions of the government and its various direct and indirect agencies. Both the academic medical centers and the IGZ are subject to directives of the National Ombudsman. There is no further recourse.

In the year I know best, the National Ombudsman dealt with 17,000 cases. Each case entailed whatever listening, probing, and researching was necessary to understand whatever might have happened. After this, the agency produced a report that included a summary and cover letter. The letter signed by the National Ombudsman was sent to the offended and offending parties; summaries and letters were also sent to the media.

One particularly sad case resulted in a strong rebuke from the National Ombudsman. The letter was based on one hundred pages of supporting information, including testimony from various people, under oath, to the National Ombudsman's staff. There was more than enough misery to go around: desperate parents; equipment issues; rushed judgments, made under pressure; regret; self-defense; and labored bureaucratic handling of the case by the IGZ.

What I saw was a human tragedy; there were no evil intentions anywhere. There was a piling up of anguish and pain and a total impossibility of righting all of the wrongs. The National Ombudsman would have had to sign fifty to one hundred such letters every working day, pointing a finger in 17,000 incidents—having barely enough time to read these letters, let alone read those one hundred pages of sworn testimony.

Those one hundred pages were well worth reading.

A bad outcome complicated the care of a very young child. The doctor in charge desperately wanted to speak to the parents to explain what had happened, how it could have happened, and how he understood their anguish and anger. He was forbidden to do so. He accepted his fate—a transfer to a small hospital—and his spirit and career were very likely broken.

The IGZ junior inspector, who wanted to justify his actions, talked about his frustrations with the superiors who kept him from doing his work.

The IGZ senior inspector in charge of the case described events, timing, and people in strikingly beautiful language with real insight, but when no useful action could be discerned, she refused to act. She would not speak out unless something helpful could be said. Her testimony alone could have served as the plot for a haunting play or opera.

In no way could the National Ombudsman's summary letter encompass all this. Although it seemed to me that the National Ombudsman had used a sledgehammer where a scalpel would have been far better, I also understood that this was, perhaps, the only way for the system to work.

An interesting country, Holland.

...

And a difficult situation to judge when your experience and accumulated wisdom have opened your eyes to all the different issues involved in such an incident.

Medical Costs

Health costs have been a major issue everywhere for at least a decade now. Politicians in the US and Europe seek solutions to keep rising costs under control, but solutions do not seem to be easily found.

Not long ago *The New York Times* wrote an editorial about a New York state hospital with a budget of $500 million. For 2010, the hospital's CEO had been paid a $4- or $5-million salary plus a bonus, having received $2- or $3-million the previous year. This was 0.5 to 1 percent of the total hospital budget. If the CEO's immediate staff received amounts that were 30 to 60 percent of their boss's salary plus bonus, management costs could quickly mount.

The large academic medical centers in the Netherlands and Switzerland have budgets that are two to three times larger than the New York hospital cited by *The New York Times*. The managements of the eight Dutch academic medical centers consist of three or four people, none of whom makes more than €350,000, including pension costs and a few fringe benefits. The fifty to one hundred specialists at each of these centers are paid between €150,000 to €200,000 each.

UMCG's nine thousand personnel (about 7,500 full time equivalents) cost around €450 million, about half the total budget. These are all reasonable numbers, contributing to the relatively modest costs of health care in the Netherlands.

• • •

Most of my European colleagues share the feeling that health care executives in the US are overpaid. Bernie makes his point with the numbers, not by editorializing.

US institutions counter with the argument that they have to offer generous pay packages in order to recruit top talent.

• • •

The situation in Switzerland differs in that there are many private clinics. For academic centers and city and cantonal hospitals, the numbers are not much different from those for the Netherlands.

About fifteen years ago, various people would ask what biotechnology hoped to contribute to this world of ours. I began looking into the economics of the industrial chemistry and pharma sectors and including some of this information in my lectures about industrial biotechnology at conferences, universities, and industries.

At one point, I discovered data on consumer expenditures accumulated yearly by the US Bureau of Economic Analysis (BEA). These turned out to be very interesting. The precursor of this bureau had collected data on total consumer expenditures since the early 1900s. The data were not very detailed, but that changed in 1959. From then on, information on three hundred expenditure categories was collected and tracked continuously in current US dollars and US dollars standardized to the year 2000 (corrected retrospectively for earlier years), with various corrections for changes in the price index applied when needed.

A nice way to look at these data was to calculate expenditures for a given category as a percentage of total expenditures, or as a percentage of the GDP, and to follow these percentages from 1959 to today. Using these percentages rather than absolute or corrected dollar figures shows changing expenditures for particular items by the average US consumer, without the need to consider inflation, population growth, or GDP growth.

Major expenditure items in 1959 were food, housing, and clothing, and together these items accounted for 50 percent of personal income. At that time, health costs accounted for 6 percent of income. This included all health-related expenses, from drugs to physicians to hospitals and even facilities for seniors. By 2009, fifty years later, food, housing, and clothing costs had decreased to 35 percent of total expenditures, while health costs had grown to 23 percent—by far the highest single item. The only other items to grow were personal services, entertainment, vacations, and such, from a total of 5 percent (1959) to 12 percent today. Surprisingly, fuel cost remained stable at about 8 percent.

Education—all of it, from kindergarten to the PhD—rose slowly from 3 percent to 4 percent in 2009.

Very generally then, the patterns seen here show that the US population went from primary needs (a roof over one's head, clothes, and food) to apparent sufficiency in this category. This is likely to be news to those who have lately lost their homes, but the percentages quoted are averages for a much larger group. The new urgent category relates not to caring for the basics (which are assumed to be available) but to more lavish care of our bodies, more enjoyment of our time on Earth, and greater attempts to avoid disease while we enjoy good times here.

How can this happen in the face of so many other needs? Clearly, the health sector differs from all other sectors. Consumers do not really have the option to refuse a loved one's urgent treatment in favor of a larger home or new car. Urgent treatments will never disappear or become unnecessary.

Back at Johns Hopkins in 1964 or 1965, we had some fine lectures from Prof. Clement Markert,[21] who left for Yale a few years later. Markert's lectures dealt with developmental biology, but he also talked about some apparently distantly related topics as well: actuarial data about disease and death. At that time, about a third of the population died of heart disease and circulatory problems, another third died of cancer, and the rest died of a variety of ailments or old age.

Markert pointed out that a graph of life expectancy for the entire population followed a nearly horizontal line from ages two to seventy, then decreased to nearly zero by age ninety. This decrease was the interesting part of the curve. One hundred years earlier, the curve had ended somewhere near the same age

---

21 One of the first American molecular biologists.

(ninety), but the decrease began much earlier, sometime around thirty or forty years.

So between 1865 and 1965, not much had happened to prolong life for the healthiest. What had happened was that more people lived longer, and because of that, the average age of the whole population had increased.

We all understood. And now for the interesting insight: Based on the data then available, when the actuaries built a hypothetical model and eliminated all heart disease, the survival curve did not change much. The slope of survival versus age remained nearly the same. What did change was that the curve moved to the right. The average age had increased by about three years.

Here, too, the message was obvious. Today, one third of the population dies of heart and circulatory diseases. If we eliminated these ailments completely, these people would still die. Some other disease would have felled them had heart disease not gotten them first.

No matter which problems are resolved and which diseases are eliminated, new limiting problems will always emerge. These, too, may be tackled and solved.

Maybe we will eliminate cancer. We will then die of something else. Would these survival curves look different? Not really. We will live longer, but only a little bit longer. Of course, the curves may be a little steeper towards the last decade before death, but die we will.

A time will come when we will have to look at the consumer expenditure curves again. Politics will not solve these problems. Doing in the voters is not likely to be a winning tactic except perhaps in rational Switzerland, where assisted suicide is legal and people come to this country to be helped just once more.

...

Bernie's retirement in 2006 ended his active participation in laboratory research and mentoring of graduate students.

Fortunately, his 2006 appointment to the UMCG's Supervisory Board provided an opportunity to focus his energies on a new set of issues. By the time of his appointment, Bernie had accumulated considerable experience as a patient. As a member of the board, he delved into understanding not just how a medical center should work but why it should work. He viewed the mission of the medical and scientific institution as a three-fold effort: education, research, and patient care.

This three-fold mission has been a central theme in academic medicine since the early days of the twentieth-century. Bernie was not an intellectual rebel; this is the party line for those who guide academic medical centers. He also gained insight from his experience with the National Ombudsman of the Netherlands; he saw the tragedy that an unexpected bad outcome creates, not just for the patient but also for the caregivers.

What is striking from his writing is that he understood the ultimate limits of the process. We generally refer to the "actuarial data" that Markert introduced as "squaring the survival curve." In very basic terms, the underlying hypothesis for the square survival curve states that, by eliminating causes of premature death (such as infectious diseases, combat, accidents, and so forth), larger and larger proportions of the human population will reach a theoretical biological maximum age before rapidly dying off. Actually, epidemiologists today recognize the importance of this squaring (or "rectangularization"). However, they also have more recent data that suggest that the absolute maximum longevity does not behave exactly as Markert stated. Instead, the probability that very old people—centenarians and older—will die in the next year becomes very high but doesn't reach 100 percent. This means there is still a tail on the survival curve.

Although we can debate the details, to quote Bernie, "But die we will." And he sensed that when our human problems ultimately become insoluble, "people come to (rational Switzerland) to be helped just once more."

CHAPTER 14

Getting Back in the Boat

Sometimes I wondered why Bernie kept at his rowing. Here's his answer.

• • •

In late spring and on towards the summer of 2008, I started using my Concept2 rowing machine again. I looked for heart rate patterns under different conditions and gradually improved my performance. I also returned to rowing on the water. I continued rowing with my ETH Zurich-eight friends; although my life at my institute was over, the eight was still there for me to try for. Mostly, however, I rowed at my Zurich club, the Grasshoppers, in pick-up crews of four and sometimes eight oarsmen. We used easy open rowing shells, almost like the training wherries that beginning oarsmen sometimes row.[22] This was always enjoyable, even when it was windy, wet, or cold or all of these. One warms up during the row. Wind and splashing water are refreshing, sometimes even exhilarating.

By the time a crew steps into a boat, they have carried it from the boathouse and set it gently upon the water. The boat is usually

---

22 In London along the tideway, wherries were water taxis; in Elizabethan times, their use was widespread.

floating alongside a dock of some sort. On one side of the boat, the oar's blades are in the water. On the other side, the oars are on the dock. Each crew member stands with one foot on the little track in the bottom of the boat. His other foot remains on the dock, ready to push the boat away.

Each rower will hold the oar's handle. (If there are two sculls, or oars, both of them are held in one hand.) With the other hand, the rower stabilizes himself or herself by holding the gunnel (the side of the boat, just twenty-five cm, or ten inches, above the waterline). Still standing, the crew pushes the boat from the dock, pulling in the dock leg while lowering onto the seat with the boat leg. The rowers settle their feet onto the footboard while wiggling their bottoms into preferred seat positions. With a few easy strokes, the crew can now move their boat into the open water, away from the dock, and fit their feet in the shoes or straps fixed to the footboards.

Some boats have coxswains; some do not. If there is a cox, he or she now gives a few commands; the rowers go through a few initial warm-up exercises, and off they go. When there is no cox, the bowman must keep an eye on traffic and the course to be rowed. This is not a trivial task. The bowman sits looking at the stern (back end) of the boat and, like all the crew in the boat, rows facing backward. With every few strokes, however, the bowman must crane his neck and turn his upper body to see what is ahead or what might be coming at the boat, without upsetting the rhythm of the crew or rocking the boat.[23]

I joined my Grasshopper friends for local longer distance events on one-day tours of Lake Lugano (in 2006), around Lake

---

23   Bernie speaks from experience; he was the bowman when we rowed a double scull.

Zurich (2006 and 2008), on Lake Constance (2007 and 2011), between the two Freiburger lakes (2009), and on the local Limmat river that flows into the Rhine (2010). We also went on longer two- or three-day tours on the Thames in England (2005), the Doubs in France (2009), the Main in Germany (2011), and around and on the Canal Grande in Venice (2012). These were all comfortable, relaxed longer distance rows (20–40 km for one-day events; 60–80 km rows for the two- or three-day events).

When my ICD was checked, we saw that from time to time, the device had recorded short episodes of tachycardia, consisting of fewer than twenty beats. These episodes had not lasted long enough to trigger a shock. If the device had sensed longer bursts, it would have charged the capacitors to deliver a shock, but the capacitors would not discharge unless the tachycardia had continued. Typically, the whole process—from sensing the tachycardia to delivering the shock—takes twenty seconds. The fact that I received very few shocks after 2001 meant that there could not have been many bursts of more than one hundred beats.

• • •

For the moment, things were going well. You can almost hear the splashing of the oars and feel the spray.

By learning to live with his tachycardia, Bernie had freed himself of many constraints. He had learned to live in the moment. Did learning to live in the moment reduce the internal stress, the "irritation," that had contributed to his vulnerability to longer episodes?

In some ways, Bernie may well have been a happier man after the onset of his tachycardia than he was before.

He particularly relished the details of getting a crew of oarsmen (often *large men) into a fragile shell. The process is choreographed, almost dainty. But if one of them slips, it's perfectly possible to put a foot through the bottom of a $20,000 boat!*

Once the oarsmen settle onto their sliding seats and strap in their feet, the whole operation is secure. For the moment.

• • •

Dating back to 1880, the Grasshopper Club (GC) was one of the old rowing clubs, with a wonderful clubhouse that was surrounded by six or seven other clubs. There were all the boats, of course. There was also a nice gym area with everything a young rower might want; eight or ten ergometers lined up in front of a long mirror, so an entire eight could admire itself and look for some sort of coordination.

Although GC has always been a men's club, ladies do join us in the boats and clubroom when they so desire. The clubroom on the second floor is magnificent. A balcony looks out over the large lawns between the boathouses and the water's edge. Half a dozen docks line the water, from which shells are launched and return after being rowed for ten, twelve, or fifteen kilometers along the southern lakeshore. The shells not in use wait in racks on the ground floor.

I often rowed with a group of GC oarsmen who had nothing to do with ETH Zurich. They were the "real" GC members; many of them had been with the club for forty or fifty years. Some had once rowed with the national squad; others had just rowed for fun and never raced. This group of so-called *breitensportler* (loosely translated as "general sportsmen") meets on Saturday mornings, and one or more crews are formed, depending on how many of us there are.

On these early Saturday morning hours, the action is almost serious as boats are rigged for takeoff. At first, there may still be a little mist on the water. An hour later, as some of the early starters come back, the mist is gone. There is laughter and fun as sweaty bodies collide while pretending to take care of the serious business of cleaning boats and hauling them back in. On sunny days, some of the returning rowers will jump in the lake, the water clear and cool.

After showering, we have breakfast on the balcony, with city views to the left and across from us on the northern side of the lake and of the Alps to the right in the east. We are close to the western end of the lake, which flows into the Limmat, the river which has surrounded the city since Roman times.

Several of the churches near the Limmat's shores date back to the 1500s. One of them, the Grossmunster, was the source of Huldrych Zwingli's reformation. This was a hardy strain of Protestantism, similar to Calvin's teachings at about the same time in Geneva, 250 kilometers to the southwest on the shores of Lac Leman (Lake Geneva). On the Zurcher lakeshore, we see the Tonhalle to the left, home to the Tonalle Orchestra Zurich, which has reached great heights in the past twenty years. Across from us, about a kilometer away at this narrow western end of the lake, are the large Seefeld Plaza and the Zurich Opera House, on par with the great German opera houses in Munich, Hannover, Hamburg, and Berlin.

• • •

How can anyone read this without smiling? Bernie's almost lyric description of his Saturday mornings went far beyond science; he loved life. He loved the experience of rowing, the athletes' efforts blending together until the boat fairly danced.

His sense of European culture and community extended beyond the rowing club—back in time to the Romans and the Reformation and across space to the "great German opera houses."

CHAPTER 15

Dearest A.C., Vince, and Kids . . .

Bernie often referred to his daughter, Anna Christina, as A.C. In this let-
ter, probably written at the end of 2007, Bernie gradually opens up to his
family about the symptoms he experienced throughout the year. He needed
five paragraphs to set the stage and another page to confess that he and his
infectious disease consultant had finally decided to do blood cultures after
he exercised. Denial, intellectualizing, stubbornness, courage . . .

• • •

Three days ago, I started writing a letter to you, which basically
recounted what has happened to me medically since early 1999.
My goal was to put together what I have experienced, learned,
read, done in the way of related experiments, and written in the
past nine years to see where there might be patterns and get a
feeling for where things might go.

I started this as a letter to you to make sure I would write it in
such a way that it would, I hope, make sense to non-biochemists
and so that it might perhaps even be useful at some point in your

lives. Putting together this "letter" may take me a few months, and so it is not a substitute for my regular mails to you.

I made an appointment with my cardiologist back in January. This was about a week after I fainted while Renske and I were walking in the snow up in the foothills, on January 1.[24] Renske came with me to the visit, and we three had a good conversation. My cardiologist made appointments for me with various other specialists. The following day, I had a CT scan done of my brain that showed no recent damage. That seemed good. On the other hand, I later asked another specialist what "recent" meant, and he looked flustered; I got no clear answer.

After the CT scan on the 11th, I was taken to the lady who had done my echocardiography examinations in 2004 and also just three months ago. She did this once more, and the echoes showed pretty much what had been seen before. Most of the indicators were a little less great or a little worse (depending on the indicator taken). So, nothing had changed dramatically, but the wear and tear on my heart seems to have continued. Also, the pace of change is greater than I would like. So, I may have to take all the advice I get and take it easy rather than trying to remain in the thick of things.

Meanwhile, I was going into shakes fairly easily. This happened perhaps once a day and from time to time at night, when I was in bed. I started wearing sweatshirts, long rowing pants, socks, mittens, and a headband plus double blankets to prevent going into the shakes, and this seemed to work.

Somewhere during this period, I realized that thinking in

---

24   It's difficult to put together the timing of these events. There's no question that the episodes of fever occurred for many months, and I suspect that this reference is to events in January 2007.

terms of external temperatures was the wrong approach. Actually, what was happening was that I lost heat, as every object does when placed in a cooler environment. So, even if you are sitting in a room warmed to 25 or 26°C, you still lose heat. It is not relevant that you might feel warm, hot, or sweaty; you will lose heat. The rate at which you lose heat depends on the insulation between you and your environment, *i.e.,* how you are dressed. One loses a lot of heat via the head. Big hair, headbands, hats, and earmuffs all reduce this loss. It feels hot when you put these things on, so when heat loss is reduced, your body tells you, "Wow, this is really comfy" or "God, this is terribly hot," and you tear off or add items until you feel right. *Feeling* right is not the same as *being* right. Your sensors or the system integrating this information in your brain may be off, like a thermostat with the wrong set of digits on the "set temperature" scale.

It is the same for socks. Once I started experimenting by adding protection/insulation, I realized how unbelievably cold my feet could feel, even though we have floor heating, and I am wearing lots of other stuff.

As a next step, I started measuring my temperature frequently and under various standard conditions. I found that, before going into shakes, I typically had cooled off to between 35.6 and 35.8°C. After a while, I was able to feel the shakes coming, and since I now knew this had to do with heat loss and a lowered temperature, I then shot into extra layers of clothing and covered every bit of skin I could. This usually caused my body to start warming up again, and the shakes either did not really get started or were mild and short-lived.

Now what about exercise and the shakes? Exercising usually warms one up. However, if one's source of total energy is limiting, and part is used for physical work, then perhaps there is not enough left to compensate for the heat that is lost to the surroundings. This is in fact what seems to happen. When I do my "yoga" set, and I check my temperature at the end of a set, it is down to 35.5°C (and sometimes lower). If I then sit and wait for a while, my body warms up to 36–36.5°C, and I do another exercise set. My body temperature goes down again, and I can warm it up by not exercising for a while. In this case I am wearing short pants and a fairly light sleeveless sweatshirt, so I can lose a lot of heat fast, but evidently my body can compensate.

Yesterday I did my exercises as usual—but perhaps a bit too vigorously—and went into mild shakes after the second set. My infectionologist [*his infectious disease consultant, or ID consultant*] and I have been hoping to get a blood sample during the shakes. This is to see if perhaps some bacteria or other microorganisms appear or reveal themselves (either as causative agents or as results). So I went to the UniSpital [*local hospital*], to have blood samples taken. Since the shakes were short-lived, my plan was to have a blood sample taken pre-exercises, then to do enough exercises to get me into shakes and have a second sample taken post-exercise.

The pre-exercise sample was easy. I then found myself a cool spot in the clinic and started off with my exercises but had no shakes. After the third set, my temperature was down to 34.2°C; I decided that was low enough, and we took a blood sample anyway, by which time I was already up to 34.8°C. I will be most surprised if the clinic finds organisms in the second sample but not in the first.

I went home by tram (couldn't find a taxi) and walked from the zoo, where the tram finishes, to our house, a walk of about 1.5 kilometers. In the tram, I had a temperature (taken, by the way, with thermometer under tongue, mouth closed) above 36°C; soon after I stepped out, it was close to 34°C. The route home has various easy ups and downs. As I expected, when I walked up (more energy needed), my temperature dropped, and when I walked down (less energy needed), it went up. Mostly it stayed between 34.2°C and 35°C. No shakes though, even though earlier they would have started at 35.6°C or so.

My present interpretation is that my heart pumps a constant, but not very large, amount of blood around my body. If I need much of my blood for muscle activity, my body does not seem capable of compensating for heat losses to the environment. When I stop the exercising, enough blood goes to organs and structures that collectively metabolize enough to compensate for heat losses.

On November 3, 2007, I rowed in the ETH "Professoren" eight (we won by a little). The previous week, I had rowed mornings and afternoons in Seville. I had the shakes one morning but adapted and was able to row a few hours later. I also had the shakes when I came home late on November 2 in a taxi, which suddenly seemed quite cold, even though I had rowed nicely that morning. The next day (November 3), I warmed up very carefully, had warm clothes with me, and we rowed our races. I had no trouble. Clearly, my heart was able to pump a lot of blood around, both to propel the boat and keep me warm.

• • •

As far as I know, this letter was the first time that Bernie told his family, other than Renske, about his "shakes." Typically, he includes his observations and theories about the shaking. His theories about fever and the physiology of temperature regulation are rather unique (certainly not what we teach in medical school). He was, however, absolutely correct about the importance of obtaining blood samples for cultures after exercise.

His letter, though, points to how hard Bernie was once again struggling to understand what was happening to him.

Here he is, a human being and a patient, refusing to abandon the role of the objective observer, continuing to gather data whenever possible. Yet he also refuses to abandon his deep denial. He's sick, having chills and fevers, and rowing through it.

CHAPTER 16

Still Rowing

As I remember, Bernie came to San Francisco sometime in mid-to-late August 2007.

I left clinical practice in 2005 to join Scios Inc., a biotech firm that had been acquired by Johnson & Johnson. This required a move to the Bay Area, and we found a home in Pleasanton, California. My wife, Katherine, and our dogs, Cody and Shadow, spent most of that summer at our cabin in Michigan's Upper Peninsula. My new job involved extensive travel, and I welcomed the prospect of having Bernie as a houseguest for a couple of days.

As we talked, he slowly let the cat out of the bag. He had lost weight. He was experiencing repeated episodes of shaking chills and fever, usually following vigorous exercise. At last, he mentioned that these symptoms had all started after an orthopedic surgeon in Zurich had done an outpatient arthroscopic procedure on his knee.

In Pleasanton, sitting in the tiny bedroom that we had converted into my home office, I had easy access to all the online medical literature one could possibly want from my corporate laptop. While Bernie, who was jet-lagged and obviously ill, napped, I searched a series of recent medical papers on PubMed, the National Library of Medicine's search service. After an hour and a half or so, I was convinced that his defibrillator lead had become infected.

I printed a copy of the best of the papers and gave it to him.[25] *The authors, from the Mayo Clinic, described 189 patients with infected pacing or ICD devices. Many of the patients, like Bernie, had only chills and fevers with very few other findings. In 60 percent of the cases, blood cultures had failed to grow bacteria. At that time, ICD infection was not widely recognized. Even when suspected, it is a very difficult diagnosis to confirm.*

I told Bernie my conclusions and recommended that he should have prompt (not emergency) hospitalization. I offered to refer him to the Cleveland Clinic to see one of my friends, Bruce Wilkoff, who is a world expert on the management of device infections.

We then decided to adjourn our medical deliberations for dinner at a local restaurant, managing to enjoy a nice bottle of wine with our meal.

The following day, Bernie politely declined the Cleveland Clinic referral. He was on the last leg of a scheduled trip, on his way home. He promised, however, that he would consult with his team of doctors in Zurich. Here's the story as he told it.

· · ·

Our yearly race, the ETH "Professoren" crew against the University of Zurich, was scheduled for October, a month after my visit with Roger.

Florian, our coach, had organized a week of rowing at the former Olympic rowing center in Seville, Spain, for the week before our race. I had more time than my fully occupied colleagues had, and I joined a mixed group of young and rather

25   Sohail MR, Uslan DZ, Khan AH et al. "Management and outcome of permanent pacemaker and implantable cardioverter-defibrillator infections." *Journal of the American College of Cardiology* 49, no. 18 (2007) 1851–9.

inexperienced rowers in Seville. We had a fine time rowing mornings and afternoons in various combinations. We all learned some technique from the videos Florian and his girlfriend made from their coaching boat as they followed our shells through Seville. It was good training, but I continued to have the shakes. They occurred once or twice during the week. We flew home on the day before the Zurich regatta and arrived late at night.

I had a severe episode of shaking in the taxi driving me home from the airport. I felt rather sorry for myself. I even considered going to the emergency room, but I knew this would undoubtedly make it impossible to take my place in the boat the next day.

"Let's see what happens," I said to no one in particular.

The next day, we did well, winning the race. After celebrating and commemorating a little, I flew to Amsterdam to attend a happening organized by my wife and one of her friends. They had set up a foundation to support art events to be shared between the Netherlands and Switzerland. Some of my friends were also there. We hung around in the hotel bar until two o'clock in the morning. Then, it seemed time to get some rest. Not very smart, but no harm seemed to result from any of this.

That changed toward December 2007.

• • •

Knowing as much as I did about Bernie's situation, I should have called Renske back in August and shared my concern. On the other hand, I was his friend, not his physician.

Friendship sometimes becomes a difficult relationship. I've talked with other doctors about similar situations. Typically, a friend asks for medical advice, and as a physician, you realize that he or she has a potentially serious problem. You ask some questions, review the literature, and try to give your friend the very best, most thoughtful advice.

And then, your friend doesn't take that advice.

I find it an impossible situation.

CHAPTER 17

Let's Get Those Bugs
into the Blood Stream!

Bernie dated these notes as "mid-January 2008."

...

I had gone back to my exercises and saw my temperatures drop-
ping to 33° and even 32°C. I continued reading about this and
that and discovered that temperatures in this lower range were
considered dangerous. Now what?

If, as I suspected, my ICD or its electrode had become infected,
I reasoned that vigorous exercise that caused my heart rate to rise
would cause my blood to flow more rapidly and possibly wash off
a few of the bacteria sitting on the device.

We can imagine that a few bacteria come along, sloughed
off the biofilm we suspect has developed either on the ICD sitting under my skin or electrodes in my vena cava connecting it
to my heart. The ICD itself is not within my circulation, but the
electrodes traverse the wall of the subclavian vein under my col-
larbone; from the subclavian, they run down the large superior
cava vein into my heart. The electrode enters my heart from the

atrium, lies across the (tricuspid) valve, and terminates in my right
ventricle. The electrode is connected to the inner wall of the ventricle with a small corkscrew-like device that extends from the
tip of the electrode. (You would like that little fellow to attach
nicely to the inner wall of your heart. Too loose a connection,
and the electrode will end up hanging free in that heart chamber.
Does that matter? What happens when you do those exercises and
move left or twist right or when somebody slaps you on the chest,
happy to have just met you again after all these years?)

The blood flow would carry these sloughed off bacteria
through my lungs, where they might end up stuck in capillaries
around the alveoli. If there were enough bacteria, a few might
make it through the lungs and into my circulation. There, they
would face my immune system, including the macrophages that
destroy bacteria and other harmful material.

Blood not only carries nutrients; with its proteins, protein
complexes, and multiple cell types, it is also the carrier fluid for
the immune system. Immunity's role is to recognize anything that
is not part of our bodies and then make sure the foreign material
is barred, inactivated, or destroyed. The problem for the immune
system, then, is to carefully distinguish "me" from "not me" and
"me" from "my environment." After we have exited our mother's uterus, the biggest challenge we face is to keep other organisms from making their way into our bodies. Bacteria and viruses,
yeasts, and parasites surround us. Immunity is what must happen to keep us safe in a whirling world of surrounding biological
material, a world of which we are an intimate part and to which
we are totally connected.

But before ever getting to one of the veins in my lower arm,
the blood entering the aorta would first feed into my arm artery

before proceeding into the branching arterial system that ends in countless capillaries that deliver blood to our cells and then return it back to the heart. The capillaries flow gradually into larger and larger vessels until finally, the bacteria would reach one of the larger veins in the lower arm, where a needle might be inserted to withdraw some of this blood. No wonder it was so hard to grow bacteria from my blood.

• • •

As the Mayo Clinic paper pointed out, 60 percent of their patients with infected ICDs had negative blood cultures. I'm still not sure that all the effort to get a positive culture was necessary.

• • •

But if our immune system does such a great job eliminating foreign material in the blood, why do a few bacteria on an electrode cause alarm?

The few bacteria that manage to get into blood are generally there in small numbers. A little bleeding along the gum's intersection with your teeth may be an entryway. If a few of the many bacteria in your mouth and on your teeth (which are most certainly there) get into the blood stream, they enter individually or in smallish clusters. The defensive molecules and cells in blood can generally get to them and eliminate them. The bugs are outnumbered—and this is all a matter of numbers. That is why a large wound from an accident or a violent encounter, which allows much more blood out and larger amounts of material in, can lead to infections so overwhelming that our natural defense systems can no longer handle this. Hence, cauterizing or cleaning with alcohol (or nastier solvents, if nothing else is available) is used to quickly eliminate all the biological life around a wound, the real haste in treating accident and war victims . . .

OK, now back to the biofilm. Why does the defense system have such problems with this? The biofilm is a layer of microorganisms, usually bacteria of various sorts, that attach to some material and grow, divide, and increase in numbers, forming new layers. After some time, a biofilm might consist of ten, twenty, thirty layers of bacteria. These are not beautiful flat layers. It is more like a few layers here, some continuing for a larger stretch, with new layers on top of the lower layer here and there. Probably a somewhat hilly environment, all these bacteria in more or less intimate contact with one another. How tightly are they packed? If the packing were too close, how would they get their nutrients from the blood flowing past? If they are too far apart, do we still have a biofilm? As always, there are local optima with lots of variation as to what is possible. When we draw a diagram, things usually look simpler and cleaner than the reality. No matter. Now imagine a large cell trying to envelop one of these bacteria. How will it do that? It is larger than the bacterium, maybe three times wider than the bacterium is long, maybe ten times higher than the bacterium is thick. It might be able to tackle a few bacteria that happen to stick together, but tackling a biofilm is more difficult. And so, the biofilm grows.

The bacteria that form a biofilm often produce and extrude various proteins and polysaccharides that end up in the immediate surrounding space. So now, the biofilm is fortified by the fact that the bacteria are, as it were, *glued* together. Not too tightly, since the layers closer to the electrodes will then not see many nutrients, but it's possible to glue things together and still leave a lot of space. This makes for a porous material that allows adequate permeation of nutrients while keeping the biofilm very much intact.

Some microorganisms create their own biofilms, even when they are floating around in a liquid medium. Two bacteria adhere to one another; a third, fourth, and more join; and soon you have a large particle that feels hard but lives and consumes nutrient. We use some of these organisms in water and waste treatment plants. They utilize and grow on various noxious chemicals in the waste and, in the process, clean the water—maybe not completely, but a long way toward desired purity. The waste has now essentially been converted into large particles that can simply sink and settle (if they happen to be heavier than water) or float (if they are lighter). They can be skimmed off or filtered out and then dumped in a landfill. The noxious chemicals have been converted to breakdown products, ultimately water and CO2. A number of industries produce plants designed to clean up industrial waste streams. It's a rather nice use of microorganisms; they are not always a threat. In fact, usually microorganisms are great friends. Believe me, I know.

How about the biofilm that happens to have formed on the electrodes sitting in my heart? It is not a friend. A number of bacteria will slough off. They will be smaller groups or individual bacteria. They will suddenly encounter massive numbers of proteins eager to attach to them. Now, these bacteria will be tagged with proteins and specialized killer cells (called macrophages) will be all around them, waiting; the killer cells will enfold these tagged bugs, effectively engulfing them. Various enzymes that attack bacterial walls and others that hydrolyze their proteins inside these killer vacuoles will finish off the bacteria as they are transported to my arms, legs, brain, and various organs. This war of destruction against the bacteria is taking place inside me, and it is what is making me sick, making me shake, giving me chills, and taking my appetite.

By the time somebody takes a sample from one of my arm veins, very few bacteria will still remain in the blood. All this suggests that blood samples should be taken as close as possible to where the presumed biofilm is located. With an infected ICD, perhaps the blood flowing into the lungs would undoubtedly reveal some organisms, even if most are still stuck together in "micro chunks" broken off the biofilm.

Another option to find the bacteria was for me to do my exercises in the hospital and have blood taken afterward, when I would develop the shaking that I experienced at home. We did this. My favorite blood-tapping lady was ready for me when, after doing a couple of exercise sets under some stairs close to the infectious disease labs, I ran over for the first tappings [*blood drawings*].

We repeated this protocol once or twice more. A few days later, Dr. Urs Karrer, my ID consultant, called me. Bacteria were growing from the blood that had been drawn after exercise. He wanted me to pack a bag and come to the hospital for the removal of my ICD and electrodes. Since there was no available room in the university's cardiology unit until the following day, he had arranged for a temporary stay at a neighboring hospital.

• • •

For practical purposes, biofilms are a result of late twentieth-century medical technology. Until we started implanting medical devices in people, no one had ever paid much attention to biofilms. Now, with artificial joints and implanted cardiac devices like valves, pacemakers, and ICDs, these infections cause widespread concern.

In this chapter, Bernie provides a graphic description of the generation of a biofilm. His powers of description came from the fact that he actually visualized it. His mind's eye could see the electrode in the dark flowing blood along with the bacteria he knew so intimately from the lab. He knew that, as long as the bacteria remained locked in their film and attached to the inanimate electrode, they would not cause symptoms. His symptoms occurred when the bacteria sloughed off and became exposed. His immune system could recognize them and then mount an attack. The fevers, chills, and shakes were the consequences of the immunologic attack.

CHAPTER 18

What to Do Now?

One of the cardinal rules of modern medicine states that if a patient's implanted device becomes infected, it must be removed to cure the infection. Thus, the critical question for Bernie and his doctors was how best to remove the ICD and electrodes.

• • •

The next day after Dr. Karrer's call, I was taken to the university's cardiology unit and told that a procedure to remove the ICD and its electrode would happen one or two days later. I found this sudden rush to get me into the hospital after I had been walking around with my bacterial buddies for a year rather amusing. The planned speedy removal I found much less amusing. I would have preferred to have my medical specialists take a little more time.

That first afternoon, several of the people who had dealt with me over the previous years came by to discuss their plans. These included Prof. Firat Duru, the successor to my first heart rhythm specialist; Dr. Candinas, who had moved to a private clinic; and Dr. Karrer, my ID consultant. Also, the heart surgeon and one of her assistants, along with the professor who headed the cardiology unit where I had been placed, came in to explain what would happen.

The surgeon, whom I had not met before, told me they would pull the electrodes out through my heart. "Minor step; we have a lot of experience with this. We go in from the side, below your left arm, and make a small incision, between the adjacent ribs. Very low risk," she said. "By the way, I will not be here; I have a conference elsewhere. My assistant will do it. Yes, lots of experience," she added. She did not say "piece of cake"; that is not standard jargon in Zurich.

I gazed at her assistant, a tall, pleasant-looking young man standing behind her. As I saw his eyes glide off into some undetermined place, I asked myself whether he had ever done this procedure before.

Dr. Karrer explained that antibiotic treatment would follow the ICD and electrode removal in order to eliminate any remaining offenders still sticking to the vein and elsewhere in my system. Prof. Duru, my heart rhythm specialist, mentioned the need to install a new ICD to protect me against future tachycardia.

They left, and I thought all this over. Given the Mayo Clinic's publication on its experience with two hundred comparable ICD and electrode removals, I was not happy about the approach described by the surgeon, nor did I like the idea of a possibly inexperienced beginner working on me.

I saw no need to have a new ICD installed. What were the chances that a new infection was more likely with a second ICD installed post-infection? This was an interesting question to be mulled over at some other time. For now, I believed I would be fine without a new ICD, just like 30 percent of the Mayo Clinic sample who had lived without the device.

I had a bad night.

I decided not to go along with the plan. If necessary, I would

pull the various tubes that restrained me out of my arm and simply leave. I could go elsewhere—to Groningen, where I was well
connected, or to one of the US hospitals that Roger had mentioned as having experts in this area.

In the morning, the head cardiologist came by and asked me
how I was. I told him of my concerns, based on the Mayo Clinic
paper. I also mentioned that things were moving too fast for my
taste. There was no hurry; a few more days (in addition to the
previous three hundred or more) were not going to be crucial.

· · ·

*In the doctor world, Bernie could sometimes qualify as a "difficult patient."
Nonetheless, his concerns were well founded. The cardiologists and the surgical team handled the situation very smoothly.*

· · ·

The head cardiologist understood, and he set up a second meeting
with the various specialists. This time, they brought along a few
relevant publications, and we agreed—there was no rush. The surgeon now said she would do the operation herself. She had just
spent a week in Stockholm observing how it was done there and
felt things would be fine here.

She agreed to start with the better procedure, namely remov-
ing the electrodes via the vein through which they had originally
been introduced. She did plan to set up everything for the second
option (pulling electrodes out through an incision in the heart) in
case the first option became problematic.

She also described the tools she had available to deal with

the electrodes. Over the eight years they'd been implanted, tissue would have formed over the electrodes, essentially incorporating them in the vein's wall. Pulling on electrodes that might be embedded in thirty or forty centimeters of the vein wall could cause serious damage. This would not be good. A Finnish company had developed a tool to deal with this concern. Its solution consisted of a flexible tube that would be fitted over the electrode being removed. The tip of this tube had a collar of small lasers that essentially burned away the tissue immediately around the electrode. This procedure allowed the surgeon to advance the tube over the electrode and free it from the vein. The goal was to do as little tissue damage as possible by having the larger tube slide over the entire length of the electrode, which could then be easily pulled out. She set up a meeting with me to review a few papers on this tool and its successful use.

I was impressed by her openness and willingness to go into this detail. I have never had any problems with intelligent and rational people who are able to shift from old positions to something demonstrably better.

We held this discussion with the doctor who would be in charge of the recovery phase; she was a young lady who I came to know as very meticulous and intelligent. It was a pleasure to be her patient.

I slept a lot better that night.

I had not enjoyed having to push back against these various specialists, but once again, doing so was essential. Pushing back was a lot better than going along, letting things happen as they might, and hoping for the best.

I found it increasingly difficult to, over and over, keep doing all this pushing back. When does one become a cantankerous old man? As the man in charge of the cardiac surgery ward said to me after these two days of encounters, "The most difficult patients are professors and other doctors." Undoubtedly true.

What is the average patient to do?

• • •

Indeed, Bernie: What is the average patient, someone who does not have your well-reasoned and polite but firm approach, to do? What happens to someone who doesn't have the scientific background you bring to your medical problems? Or, who is less suited than you to take on the role of cantankerous old man?

All I can offer are two answers based on my own experience as a patient and a physician.

First, it is always preferable to be under the care of a fairly busy doctor. Those who are not busy may well be hungry to perform lucrative procedures. Those who are too busy may not give their undivided attention. But those who are moderately busy have no motive to do unnecessary procedures and are almost always good at what they do. It's another Goldilocks problem: not too cold, not too hot, but just right.

Second, no doctors who are proud of their work and comfortable with their professional judgments would refuse to make referrals for second opinions. In fact, if you ask for a referral, those doctors will probably recommend someone who is a recognized expert on your particular problem.

Bernie's peculiar talent for debating issues without hostility stood him in good stead during this episode.

CHAPTER 19

Pre-Operative Testing

I went through some additional tests before the ICD and electrodes were removed.

One was a coronary arteries check. These arteries supply blood to the heart to enable it to contract and carry out its pumping activity.

I was prepared to check my coronary arteries and their neighboring vessels. This is done by injecting a contrast fluid into one of the major blood-supplying arteries, and this fluid then spreads through the arterial network around the heart. The contrast fluid can be seen very nicely with X-ray machines that rotate around the body; the images displayed on screens clearly show how the contrast fluid spreads through the network. Vessels' dimensions are quite clearly shown, so that any narrowing or aneurisms (where a vessel blows up locally, usually as a result of the internal pressure on weakened vessel walls) can be easily seen.

No aneurisms or blockages of the coronary arteries were revealed, which I was happy to hear.

I did, however, learn quite a lot about the coronary arteries. People at risk of a heart attack often know about their condition and carry some emergency medication, like nitroglycerin. Nitroglycerin expands the coronary arteries, including the portion that may have caused the reduced blood flow. This provides some relief.

Another approach was developed by a fellow named Andreas Gruentzig at the very same cardiology department of the University of Zurich medical school and hospital where I have been a frequent visitor these past thirteen years. This is the stent, a little collapsible tubular frame that is mounted on a catheter. Within the collapsed stent is a little balloon at the end of the catheter. Using a guide wire, the catheter can be manipulated into a coronary artery and maneuvered to the narrowed location that is causing the chest pain.

After being located at the target position, the stent is expanded by inflating the little balloon. Then the balloon is deflated, and the catheter and balloon are removed. This leaves an expanded stent in place and ensures that the inner diameter of the coronary artery is once again normal. Blood flow is also normal, and the heart functions once more as it should. This technology has been improved and refined over the past three decades, and there are people who have two, three, and more stents in the coronary arteries around their heart, living perfectly normal lives as a consequence of these very useful devices. Quite a feather in the cap for Zurich.

• • •

Andreas Gruentzig was born in Germany in 1939, but his pioneering work was, indeed, done in Zurich. He revolutionized the clinical practice of cardiology. He was a hero to the first generation of so-called interventional cardiologists.

• • •

Another pre-operative examination was yet another echocardiogram. The major reasons for doing these examinations are to measure the volumes of the different heart chambers and the thickness of the external walls. The echocardiogram also provides dynamic information about the pumping function of the atria and ventricles, and the status (narrowed or leaky) of the various heart valves. When the left atrium contracts, blood should flow forward into the ventricle. Similarly, blood ejected from the left ventricle should flow forward into the aorta, not back into the left atrium, where it had just been. Finally, blood that had been pushed through the aortic valve into the aorta should flow on to the body and not leak back into the ventricle.

One additional important piece of data about heart function measured from the echocardiogram is the ratio of the volume of blood ejected by the ventricle as compared to the volume of this same ventricle. This ratio is known as the ejection fraction (EF). For healthy people younger than sixty years old, this number is usually 70–72% for men and 74–75% for women. EF is an important number because if it decreases, the heart has to beat faster to pump a given volume of blood per minute. EF values as low as 55% are considered acceptable—and even at 45%, there need not be major concerns. When this number drops below 35%, however, the heart delivers only half the blood volume per minute delivered by a normal heart that is beating at the same rate. At this point, there is concern, and various corrective measures need to be considered: medication that might address the problem; a significant slowdown of physical exertion; perhaps replacing ineffective valves that no longer prevent backflows of blood; and in extreme cases, when EF drops below 20%, a heart transplant.

My echocardiogram data were so-so, as they had been since

the first measurements in 2000. My EF was usually around 45% and not really worrisome, though 60–65% would have been much better. With an EF of 70%, I would have been where the average male tends to be. The other numbers did not mean much to me but began to interest me later that spring.

• • •

Inappropriate emphasis on the ejection fraction, particularly as a reason to consider heart transplantation, has probably caused more anxiety for patients with heart disease than any other topic.

The ejection fraction is a ratio; it doesn't mean "my heart function is only 35%" (or whatever the number may be). Hearts with reduced EF usually show some degree of compensatory dilation, so that the heart pumps a smaller fraction of a larger number and maintains near-normal flow (at least at rest).

Surprisingly, Bernie did not apply his usual mathematical rigor to the issue of his EF. Perhaps it was too close to home. The ejection fraction is a relative, not absolute, measure of cardiac performance. A normal heart with a resting left ventricular volume of 100 ml or so and an ejection fraction of 60% will eject 60 ml with each heartbeat. A malfunctioning heart that has dilated to a left ventricular volume of 200 ml with an EF of 30% will also eject 60 ml with each heartbeat. The malfunctioning heart has a lower ejection fraction but compensates to maintain the same output by enlarging its resting volume. Though there are many adverse consequences to this compensatory mechanism, resting cardiac output does not usually fall until late in the course of heart failure.

Bernie's writing shows that the ejection fraction issue deeply concerned him.

. . .

There may have been an additional scan of some sort. If there was, the results were not noteworthy.

. . .

When we are at rest, our brain normally uses about 10 to 15 percent of the blood flow. When we use our brain, more blood will be needed there. For those of us interested in losing weight while continuing to eat as we ate before, increased activity (such as exercise) has been reported to work nicely. Serious wishful thinking might actually do the same with the brain; this is probably one of the very few cases where thought helps achieve a desired goal. Thinking hard about other things is, of course, probably equally effective.

If the brain receives too little oxygen, it will begin to sustain damage. It is usually assumed that if the brain receives little or no oxygen for more than four minutes, there will be serious brain damage; this damage, of course, increases with increasing time. Since enzymatic processes in brain cells cause the damage, and enzyme processes are temperature dependent, the damage occurs more slowly at lower temperatures. Some twenty or thirty years ago, the medical world realized that drowning victims who had fallen in very cold water could be successfully resuscitated as long as twenty minutes after falling in and apparently dying. As long as the heart and lungs could be reactivated, brain damage was actually relatively minor due to the low temperature.

Something similar might happen to people who, due to an obstruction of the coronary arteries, lose the normal flow of

blood to the heart muscles. One might surmise that it is better
to have a heart attack in a cold rather than nicely warmed house
and that there is likely to be more damage associated with heart
attacks in the summer than winter (at least for those heart attacks
that happen outside).

• • •

*Who else would have speculated on the metabolic effects of wishful think-
ing on weight loss?*

*Does Bernie's interest in the effects of cold-water immersion on slow-
ing brain damage give a clue to his unspoken concerns about himself? In
some quiet moments, had Bernie thought about what would happen if,
while rowing, he developed a tachycardia, lost consciousness, and fell out of
the shell and into the cold water?*

*Bernie was certainly aware of the link between changes in environ-
mental temperature and the metabolic demands of his microorganisms;
extrapolating those changes to his brain was not a stretch.*

Tachycardia and Heart Attacks

Tachycardia is different from heart attacks. With tachycardia, the
problem is the rate at which the heart tries to do its work. The
heart rate increases so much that the pumping action of the atria
and ventricles at each beat is ineffective, and less blood flows into
the arterial system. With too little blood flowing into the system,
vital organs stop functioning: first, the brain and then, the heart.
Things are now at a standstill but not yet terminated.

For the tachycardia patient, the heart rate must be brought
down. This can be done with drugs, but if the patient has already

fainted, drugs do not work rapidly enough to prevent brain damage. Hence, we see increasing numbers of automatic external defibrillators (AEDs) in public places like airports, stadiums, restaurants, and more. Bystanders can use these AEDs to administer a shock to someone who has had a tachycardia. The devices work almost automatically, independent of the person connecting the device to a tachycardia patient.

· · ·

Bernie was an informed patient, certainly. He also did not hesitate to push his own viewpoint. His comments about the public availability of AEDs support his plan to forego another implant after his infection had been treated. It really is not a very good argument, unless Bernie had secretly planned to live in an airport or a stadium.

CHAPTER 20

Is It Useful to Implant a New ICD?

Late January and early February 2008.

. . .

A few days later, my ICD and electrodes were removed. The surgeon came by the day after the procedure; she said she had been able to extract the electrodes after dislodging them from the vein with the laser-tipped tube. She had had to pull harder than expected, but the procedure had worked well enough. Both the ICD and electrodes were coated with bacterial biofilms.

Prof. Duru, my second heart rhythm specialist, came by several times to discuss the implantation of a new ICD, something that did not particularly interest me. I did believe I needed some sort of safety device but had already decided I would buy an AED. This turned out to be somewhat problematic because the device sold to the public differs from that used by professionals. The public version is totally automated and designed to be applied by a helpful bystander, not by the patient, in the home or public places. The assumption is that victims of tachycardia could well have lost consciousness and would not be able to apply the chest electrodes or, even if they had, might not be able to activate the device.

I was, in any case, more interested in a professional unit with options to vary some parameters. Prof. Duru set up a meeting with a small Swiss company that builds relatively portable AEDs. We had an interesting discussion on the workings of their machine, likelihood of its need from time to time, and its ease of operation while one has a tachycardia. One of Prof. Duru's coworkers was also present at this meeting. After the meeting was over and we'd planned a follow-up meeting to decide how to proceed, the coworker stayed and took me to task.

Once again, I was confronted by an intelligent young professional who disagreed strongly with all that these three experts (specialist; portable AED manufacturer; and I, the patient), had been happily debating and planning. As usual, I could only respect her for the clarity of her viewpoint, logic of her reasoning, and conviction that her conclusions were right and important. She felt that the only way to deal with a serious tachycardia was to go to the nearest emergency room and professional team able to take appropriate medical action and ready for any complications that might arise. These were all things a patient-operated AED absolutely did not offer. Using it when it is the only alternative made sense, of course, but using an AED when far better options are available is, well, just plain stupid. She probably did not use those exact words, but it was unquestionably clear that this was what she meant.

. . .

This little vignette could have been titled "The Emperor's New Defibrillator." Yes, Bernie, you got it! She was telling you that the idea was "just plain stupid." I agree with her.

• • •

I believe we had a second meeting, and I seem to recall she was not there. I can well imagine "Why waste time on this bunch?" may have been her thinking. Nothing much came of any of this talk. Meanwhile, I had found a small US manufacturer that produced a vest with a built-in AED, ready for action as needed. An extracorporeal version of an internal ICD, the vest looked like something that folks who hold traffic signs for highway construction might wear. I thought this made a lot of sense. There was no need to have an implant, no risk of infections, no problems with battery replacement, and a much, much lower cost. Though when compared to the almost invisible ICD, the modest bulk of the bright yellow vest might be a slight disadvantage, but this seemed a meaningless point to me.

• • •

The wearable defibrillator Bernie described, marketed as the Zoll Life-Vest, has evolved over the years but is still available. Electrophysiologists do use them to allow a patient whose condition is not yet considered stable to be discharged from the hospital and recover safely at home. With this idea, Bernie was a few years ahead of his time.

• • •

In the end, I bought none of the external devices, nor did I have a new ICD installed. I am still checked once a year by Prof. Duru, and he always brings up the question of the missing ICD; perhaps this is because professional responsibility requires Prof. Duru to note in the report that, despite the risks of living without an ICD, the patient has once again refused to consider a new implant. Fine.

. . .

Bernie had decided to go home without the ICD. He began to think about whether or not it provided any benefit when he realized it had not discharged very often since 2001. He did not factor in the risk of the many short episodes of tachycardia that were detected but not shocked, the importance of his regular use of the antiarrhythmic medications, and his flecainide and metoprolol succinate dosages. Nor did he account for the fact that he had learned how to manage his exercise program to avoid periods of vulnerability.

Doctors and patients alike have problems with medications that are taken in order to prevent problems. As long as the problem does not occur, there is just no way to know if these drugs are working. Maybe the problem would never have happened; maybe it has "gone away." In either case, the effort, expense, and side effects of continued treatment would no longer be justified. Of course, if you stop the preventive treatment and then have the problem, you were wrong.

These are difficult discussions, particularly with patients who are facing essentially lifelong treatment. In most situations with a high likelihood that the patient's problem is merely suppressed, not cured, continued preventive treatment offers the best outcome.

Since an ICD's battery life is limited, there are always options to discontinue treatment, either by simply turning it off or by not replacing it when the batteries are depleted.

Bernie had required multiple previous shocks. In this situation, when a functioning ICD had been removed for infection, most cardiologists would strongly advise its replacement.

• • •

After the operation to remove my ICD and a second operation to clean up some of the lingering results of this removal, it was now time to eradicate the remaining offending microorganisms. It turned out that my particular *Staphylococcus* (coagulase-negative) was susceptible to only a few antibiotics, and I was quite allergic to two of these.

Soon after my ICD and the electrodes had been removed, I was started on a cocktail of penicillin, rifampicin, and vancomycin, administered orally and via infusion. After a few days, red spots covered my body; the eruption intensified as time passed. The dermatologists performed multiple biopsies and concluded I had a rather serious penicillin allergy. My immune response was causing damage to the inner skin layers. Penicillin was taken off the program; a substitute was needed.

This was interesting. If we are lucky enough to have an effective antibiotic against a given infection, we now come to a second filter. We need an antibiotic that can destroy the offending bacterium and at the same time, does not affect us. I had never encountered this before, so I'd not considered the possibility I would run out of available antibiotics—not because they didn't exist but because my body couldn't deal with them.

Fortunately, daptomycin, a new penicillin derivative, was available (although it is still somewhat experimental). It cost CHF 250 (250 Swiss francs) per daily dose. I received sixty or so doses of daptomycin by infusion without further allergic reactions.

It took about thirty to forty minutes to administer a full dose of the antibiotic directly into my blood stream by dripping it slowly into a vein. This kept me in the hospital longer than I liked. After a week or so, I was able to go home for much of the day but was expected back in my hospital bed by ten o'clock at night. After another week, I was discharged but continued going to the hospital for my daily infusion. This lasted for another six weeks before the bugs could not be found in my blood. Of course, this in itself did not prove all that much, since the bugs weren't detected earlier when I was clearly facing zillions of the little bacterial beasties.

When I began walking around again, I felt much like I had felt in the first year after the tachycardia had started. It was difficult to walk more than fifty meters without stopping, standing still for a while, and recovering somehow.

This did not make much sense. I was taking my flecainide and metoprolol succinate as usual, but I felt much as I had felt in the pre-flecainide days. Various tests were made, including an echocardiogram.

I was not happy to learn that the EF of my left ventricle had decreased from the earlier 45% (not a very good number) to 30% after the ICD removal. This was now only less than half the normal pumping function.

The gentleman who operated the echo equipment cheerfully informed me this was not that bad; they only started to recommend a heart transplant when they saw an EF of less than 20%. I do not remember whether I was still able to laugh heartily about this information. Probably not. On the whole, I still felt quite happy. The nurses were helpful and cheerful; the young doctor whom I dealt with most often was highly competent. I found her thoroughness and intelligence very impressive.

· · ·

Bernie's serious concerns about the further decrease in his heart muscle function after the ICD extraction show through his protestations of being "quite happy."

On top of the surgical extraction procedure he'd just undergone, given his severe allergic reaction to the initial antibiotics and prolonged course of IV daptomycin, this news about his heart was very discouraging.

Once again, Bernie had to find a way to deal with it, and once again, his favored method was self-experimentation. But first, he needed an extended intellectual walkabout to deal with some of the stress. Come along and just enjoy this bit of a diversion; the next chapter showcases his enthusiasm for teaching.

CHAPTER 21

Lecture:
Infections and Antibiotics

In 1650, a Dutch lens maker produced a new type of magnifying instrument and first saw bacteria and yeast. Antonie van Leeuwenhoek, the lens maker, used this little device—what came to be called a microscope—to look at various materials, including water from the canals in Delft, his hometown. Leeuwenhoek made drawings of the tiny objects that sometimes seemed to move around in the droplet of water he was looking at with his new microscope. Someone, possibly a faculty member of Leiden University,[26] advised him to send his drawings to the Royal Society in London. Although there is no documentation that van Leeuwenhoek could write (and, what's more, write in English), the Royal Society did receive his drawings.[27] They can be seen in several publications from that time. There was great speculation about what these objects might be, where they came from, and what, if anything, they did.

---

26 Leiden University, founded a century earlier, was twenty kilometers from Delft (a good hike in those days but not impossible).

27 Bernie, a distinctly modern European, appears to have forgotten that Latin was the scientific language of the seventeenth century.

Microorganisms

Early microbiologists (who, of course, were not aware that this was what they were, since they, like other early scientists, simply became interested in various mysteries) began to think about the distinction between inanimate and living matter. Some of this thinking occurred in the 1700s, but it was only in the mid-1800s that it became clear that life did not arise spontaneously. Life, as it turned out, arose only in an environment that had been previously seeded with life.

Louis Pasteur, a French chemist, showed that by adding sugar and a few salts to clean water in a flask closed with a good stopper (perhaps cork or wad of cloth) and then boiling this solution, no living organisms could inhabit the flask—even after waiting for several months. But when he added some particles from the bottom of large vats used to brew beer, something did happen. After a while, more of these particles appeared in his flask.

There had been a spirited discussion about these particles in the beer vats. The discussion went on for at least fifty years, with experiments done by Justus von Liebig and others. They had concluded that some sort of self-generation was going on, since there were more particles at the end of the fermentation than when fermentation had started. These early scientists tried to determine what these particles were; gradually, they developed methods to identify exactly what fermentation produced. Much of this early chemical analysis was, in fact, all about the discovery that biological matter was, in fact, chemical in nature. Biological material was not something special; it was not different from chemical material. Biological material seemed different only because it was generally more varied and complex than most of the chemicals scientists had already studied.

With more chemical insight and better techniques and tools for chemical analysis, early microbiologists began to look for microorganisms. And they found them everywhere: in water; in the beer, wine, and cheese production processes; within animals, plants, and soil; everywhere they looked. Soon, microbiologists began classifying the organisms, peering into their insides, and analyzing their chemical composition. Gradually, differences emerged. Names were given to specific organisms based on where they were found for instance—on plant roots or animals' skin, in soils or in salt water, and wherever. When microorganisms were found in people or animals with a specific disease, these creatures were named after the diseases they'd apparently caused. Microorganisms might also be named by their size and shape, or for what they needed to grow, or for the chemicals they produced.

Life Sciences—Progress

This is how microbiology, biochemistry, genetics, molecular biology, physiology, and other life sciences developed. Some known organism turns out to have a unique property; something unusual happens when a new protein molecule is added to bacteria or human cells grown in the laboratory. We see new functions, though we do not usually see new structures. So, we name new organisms after their functions.

Later, we begin to work out the molecular or chemical basis and learn which molecules carry out these functions. For people who do not live in the life scientist or medical practitioner's world, these words have no particular meaning. But to workers in this complex business, these describe processes and behaviors. If we happen to be specialists in some particular tiny area within this marvelously complex and universal biosystem, we also know something about the structure and differences between seemingly related names: objects, organisms, enzymes, and DNA sequences, on and on.

The verbiage is usually lots of fun, but sometimes, it is unnecessarily complex. Don Brown, the best teacher of organic chemistry I have encountered, finally clarified some of the field's mysteries during my early graduate school days at Hopkins. He said, "It's just to keep the riff-raff out. We're just people, like everybody else, hanging on to our particular little specialness . . . "

More about Microorganisms

As we learned more about these microorganisms, it became clear that one group was very small—so tiny, the organisms are barely visible with a modern microscope—and another was relatively larger. Once the microscopes were good enough to clearly distinguish shapes and take measurements (sort of), we could make distinctions; spherical microorganisms with diameters of one or two micrometers stood apart from longer, tubular, cigar- or banana-shaped types. These were perhaps two to four micrometers long and had half to one micrometer diameters or widths. They have volumes of around one to two or three cubic micrometers. (One micrometer is one millionth of a meter, which is equivalent to about one 2.5 millionth of an inch.) Even these "big" little fellows are quite small, and you can pack around a trillion of them on the tip of your pinky.

Despite these microorganisms' very small size, they have great capabilities. They can live in bunches and in isolation. They may float around in the world's oceans (those we call, not illogically, marine bacteria). Others can adhere to surfaces: rocks in river beds; our teeth and skin; almost any available surface, such as the polymeric coating of an ICD's electrodes. They live wherever the nutrients necessary for their survival are found, which is to say, almost everywhere. Microorganisms are quite modest in their needs. Many need no more than a single type of sugar molecule and a few salts to produce every single molecule to construct an entire bacterium: all its DNA; all its RNA; all those different proteins, vitamins, polysaccharides, lipids, and various odds and ends their own best function requires. The vast majority of the different bacteria around us either do not bother us or do good and useful things. A cow lives by eating grass but cannot digest the grass. So, the cow has several stomachs, one of which is filled with bacteria that breaks down the grass cells, releasing all of the molecules in this grass. Once the bacteria have done their job, the grass molecules are available to produce whatever is needed to repair and create the molecules that go into making the cells and tissues, which together, constitute a cow.

When people sweat, we release not only water and some salts but also fats and lipids. Bacteria that live on and in the outer layers of the skin in our armpits use these. They grow on these exuded compounds and, in the process, produce new compounds with various odors. Depending on our state—resting, exerting, nervous, scared, whatever—these odors may differ, and we and others might like them (or not). This suggests that the composition of these exuded compounds differs under different conditions. It's also possible there are various microorganisms that live in our armpits. Depending on our physical or emotional state, certain bacteria grow better than others, which changes the composition of the compounds they produce and alters the odor of the products.

Our gut is populated by many different organisms. With all

of the modern technologies available today, about seven hundred different types have been identified. Each of us appears to carry around three hundred of these different bacteria and perhaps other microorganisms. Thus, we each have our specific bacterial gut ecosystem. The species composition of this ecosystem may also be related to our foods. So, our own internal ecology might influence how we deal with the foods we eat.

From time to time, undesired bacteria come along and become a part of one of these ecosystems. This may have undesirable consequences. Our bodies will want to get rid of these strangers and our immune system is generally able to do so. Sometimes, however, that is not the case; at that point, it is nice to have additional tools to get rid of unwanted organisms. In the late 1800s and first half of the 1900s, when little or nothing was known about the details that caused various infections and infectious diseases, one approach was to manage infections and infectious diseases with changes of environment. For example, physicians sent tuberculosis patients to clinics in the Swiss mountains in the hope that sunshine and fresh air might help them recover. Only relatively wealthy people could afford such treatments. For the rest of the population, at least until the early 1940s, bacterial infections were usually managed with hope and prayers. Better alternatives were needed.

How to Find Bacteria: Looking for Microorganisms

A solid-looking layer of agar, a cultural medium for growing bacteria that is derived from seaweed, is actually mostly water with a little agar mixed in. The agar forms a gel in a little dish, with a nice even surface, so that one can now add other things on top of the agar layer. If one adds 2% agar to the water—or twenty grams of agar to one thousand grams of water (which is the same as adding twenty grams of agar to one liter of water, a little more than a quart of water)—and boils this mix, the agar melts to create a nice liquid that looks a little like apple juice. When the boiled liquid cools below about 45°C, the liquid solidifies. Before this happens, we usually pour the liquid in shallow dishes, after which the agar solidifies and we now have a nice flat and uniform surface. If we use only 1% agar, we still get this flat surface, but it is a little blubbery, like Jell-O or the jellies our mothers made back in the old days. In fact, jellies form in the same way but use gelatin instead of agar. Gelatin is a protein, which is part of cartilage, a material that is related to bones, and is in fact obtained by processing slaughterhouse wastes. Gelatin has been used for the same purposes we use agar today.

Agar has the advantage that it remains solid when reheated, whereas gelatin simply melts again. This means that it can be kept warm and grow bacteria. If we now take some water that contains a few bacteria and spread it over an agar plate or Petri dish, the bacteria stick to the surface. Since the agar layer contains a variety of nutrients needed by the bacteria, they will utilize these, grow, and then divide. This happens very quickly. If they have everything needed to grow well, some bacteria can grow and divide in half an hour. After one hour, bacteria present after half an hour have again grown and divided, so we now have four bacterial cells. Each of these grows and divides again, resulting in eight of these bacteria in the next half hour and sixteen after only two hours of this growing and dividing. Four after one hour, sixteen after two, sixty-four after three, 256 after four, 1,024 after five, and so on—all starting with a single cell. By ten hours, we have more than a million cells; after another five hours, we are up to a billion cells. On and on this goes.

These cells pile up, and when there are a billion or so, we
have a clearly visible pile, which microbiologists call a colony. So,
for every single bacterium in the few droplets of water we put on
an agar plate yesterday afternoon, we now see a colony. If we had
one hundred bacteria, we will see one hundred colonies (possibly
less, if a few do not get going). If all of the bacteria are identical, we'll see identical colonies—about the same size and color,
with the same surface characteristics. If the original one hundred
bacteria are not identical, we may see different types of colonies.
The more rapidly growing bacteria might form larger colonies.
Colony color, shape, and surface properties may all differ.

To see whether a blood sample contains bacteria, the microbiology technician "plates" it, meaning a small amount of blood
is spread over the agar. Sometimes, the blood is first mixed with
water or water that might contain a few different compounds
(salt, whatever). If the blood contains fifty bacteria, many different
colonies will be seen the next day. If the technician is experienced, it's possible to identify some of the bacteria in the blood
simply by looking at the colonies formed. Today, there are various tests to identify many different bacteria so the few bacteria
finally found could be determined to be a *coagulase-negative Staphylococcus*. My bugs were evidently similar to the major group of
bacteria identified in the Mayo Clinic paper based on some two
hundred cases associated with infected ICDs and electrodes that
I described earlier.

Fleming and Penicillin

The story of Alexander Fleming's chance discovery of penicillin in 1927 is well known. It is a great example of the power of

serendipity. The experiment was not planned, and its results were totally unexpected.

Fleming had plated some bacteria in a petri dish that contained a solid layer of agar. Perhaps Fleming wanted to see if all colonies were identical or use these colonies for some analytical purpose. Whatever he'd intended to study, he had not planned for a fungus to fall onto one of his agar surfaces before he closed the plate. That wayward fungus may have been attached to a dust particle; it may have been wafted in when somebody opened a door before Fleming replaced the lid on his petri dish. Whatever the source of this fungus, it too developed a colony on that plate, and those individual fungal cells within this colony did what fungi do: They metabolized the medium Fleming had added to the agar before he poured his plates. The individual fungi grew larger, divided, and formed new fungal cells. These cells not only produced the molecules necessary for their growth; they also extruded various molecules into the surrounding environment. Some of these extruded molecules were toxic to other microorganisms, among them various bacteria. Evidently the production of such toxic compounds had been advantageous to the fungus. It reduced the number of surrounding bacteria—bacteria that would otherwise have consumed fuel and molecules the fungus needed for itself. Evolution gave the fungus not only the tools to reproduce but what it required to improve its chances of survival in competitive environments with other living organisms.

What Fleming noticed is that there were no bacterial colonies close to the fungal interloper. He had not added the fungi to his plate intentionally, but they were there and they did what fungi do. Farther away from the fungi, Fleming could see some bacterial colonies. They were smaller than he was accustomed to seeing under normal conditions. Those colonies that were farthest away were almost normal-sized. Evidently the fungus produced some chemical compound that travelled through the agar in all possible directions. It could not penetrate very far, since the agar layer was probably no more than one centimeter deep. It could probably not go up, out of the agar, unless it were a small molecule that formed a gas (such as CO_2). What it could do was diffuse laterally, over the entire surface of the plate. Under these conditions, the highest concentration of this compound would be near the fungus and become less as the compound diffused farther from the fungus. And so it was that bacterial colonies close to the fungus were exposed to a higher concentration of this compound, whereas the concentration of the compound farther away was lower; bacteria close to the fungus grew more slowly, forming small colonies, while those farther from the fungus grew faster, close to their normal growth rate, and formed larger colonies. All this came from a little mistake—some dirt falling onto the plate's surface.

Fleming understood what he had seen and then tried to identify the compound responsible for these effects. The fungus responsible for its production was *Penicillium notatum,* and so, even before its chemical structure was known, Fleming named the compound "penicillin." This is another example of a compound isolated, function found, and name given, with the detailed chemical structure worked out later.

This compound's potential was obvious to Fleming. How to bring it into the clinic; how to begin using it for practical purposes? That would require resources far beyond anything available to him in the late 1920s. All of this changed dramatically when World War II began. Only twenty-five years earlier, more British soldiers had died in World War I from infection than from cannon and rifle fire.

The remedies available then were totally inadequate. With the onset of World War II, a huge American pharmaceutical project to begin producing penicillin in large quantities was set up, and within two years, the compound was generally available to army units in the field. It was made using the same fungus originally found by Fleming, which had been steadily improved in Florey's Oxford laboratory using classical techniques. Antibiotics, so-called because they act against bacteria, fungi, and parasites, are wonderful molecules.

Louis Pasteur said, "Chance favors the prepared mind" (or something close to that when translated from French). Stories like that of Fleming and penicillin still occur. One of the major research areas in my lab began around 1980. It was based on a mistake by one of my students, a big mistake. Instead of throwing everything in the garbage can and starting again, she decided to let the experiment continue. The results were diametrically opposite from everything I'd told her to expect. She spent the rest of her doctorate training following this new thread, and dozens of other PhD students have since continued her work.

Students love to show their professors were mistaken. The good students also love to follow their own notions; they hate to be told what to do. Those who seek support and help at every turn do not become good researchers. So, as a teacher or research advisor, one points students in some direction but allows them to make the work theirs. The process does not take long. Within a few months, students will explain their thinking on this direction. There's no need for the professor to do more than smile a little and provide an environment in which students can explore their own ideas.

Good students also take responsibility for their own failures. They stimulate one another, perhaps even fight among themselves.

Their ups and downs can be hard. But teaching is a wonderful process, one that involves much more than simply training
another life scientist. When all goes as it should, the result is one
more person who is now able to take apart a problem, put it
into manageable components (each to be solved in its way), and
reassemble a plausible solution. I see no great difference between
today's academic research environment and an Italian painter's
atelier in the 1400s; the learning process is the same.

ICDs and *Staphylococci*

The fact that all of these bacteria have the same designation
(*coagulase-negative Staphylococcus*) does not really mean they are all
completely identical, any more than the description "Chevrolet,
green" indicates we are dealing with one specific car. But at least
there is some resemblance. To narrow this down, we can always
send samples of the bacteria we want to know more about to various national laboratories, which try to catalogue all the bacteria
seen in hospitals, universities, and industrial microbiology laboratories. We also send samples to other microbiologists, who can
then compare all the green Chevys more closely to differentiate
between models, engine configurations, production years, and so
on. It might then turn out that the *coagulase-negative Staphylococci*
found on ICDs and electrodes are in fact identical, or they are all
quite closely related. If so, how could that be? How does a bug
that hits Americans in various Western and Midwestern locations
spanning more than a decennium also hit me in Switzerland?
Why not all the other bacteria I've been in contact with that
might somehow have gotten into my blood?

Maybe many bacteria have gotten into the blood of all of

these different ICD carriers. However, only one group, a set of closely related *Staphylococcus* (all *coagulase-negative*), tends to adhere better to the electrode or ICD surface, or both. This particular organism escaped attacks by my immune system through its ability to form a biofilm.

Where did this bug come from? Did we all already carry it? Was it perhaps already on the electrodes or ICD when these were implanted? How could that be? The implants were presumably sterilized and packaged under sterile condition with no bugs anywhere near. The sterile packs were opened carefully and inserted into these various bodies with utmost care. Everything was fine when the surgeons closed the insertion wound, suturing and bandaging before sending those patients back to their rooms—or even homes, since these rather simple procedures are sometimes carried out in a polyclinic under local anesthesia.

Microorganisms in Hospitals

But people with infections or infectious diseases go to hospitals. They are treated by nurses, paramedics, and physicians. Bugs can be transferred from a patient to a few objects nearby. Though this is never intended, it is well known that any hospital's doorknobs, cart handles, and other surfaces often carry many different microorganisms. Hospital staff is required to wash hands after using toilets, and most believe they do so. However, more objective studies show that this often does not happen. A 70 percent incidence of failure to wash up after bathroom visits has been reported. This is true for both large Dutch and US medical school hospitals. There seems to be little reason to expect that these cases were exceptions.

Are these bugs really a problem? Maybe not. We seem to be

pretty hardy, with generally good immune response systems. If no bugs could be identified in blood samples in about half the infected ICD cases, this suggests that the bugs that did leave the heart were dealt with before they could be recognized in the blood returning via arm veins just a few minutes after having left the heart.

When the immune system is not functioning properly, things change. People with AIDS (acquired immune deficiency syndrome) have lousy immune defenses and are susceptible to infections and infectious diseases that most of us happily defeat. Before the advent of antiretroviral drugs, these patients used to die from the fact that they were easy prey for all sorts of common bugs that coexist with us, not from AIDS itself.

As it turns out, hospitals are the repositories for high concentrations of all sorts of microorganisms our systems do not often see. In the hospital, we find a population of patients who carry an immense range of pathogenic organisms—precisely that rare set that cause difficulties. As the patient population in the hospital turns over, the departing people leave some of these organisms behind to be picked up by other patients and hospital personnel. Immunologically-intact individuals, such as the personnel, do not appear to suffer much, but patients with weaker immune defenses risk being infected with new and undesirable organisms.

More about Antibiotics

Twenty years later, I spent a summer doing some analytical and modest research work at the Gist- en Spiritusfabriek in Delft, Holland. At that time, the facility produced about 40 percent of penicillin manufactured worldwide. It had improved the capability of major penicillin-producing fungi many thousandfold. The production of penicillin G was a fine example of an early industrial biotechnology process.

Another thirty years later, just a few years after the Berlin wall fell, I was asked to serve as a scientific advisor to the Hans Knöll Institute (HKI) in Jena, Germany, an East German (DDR) institute dating back to the 1930s. During World War II, HKI had also developed large-scale penicillin production processes based on strains and information stolen from Fleming's laboratory. As a result, Nazi Germany possessed the same penicillin that was available to the Allied powers. This is one more example of how fast we are able to do difficult things when stakes are truly high. Today, a similar development would take a decade or more, partially because of more stringent regulations (quite understandably) and the economic constraints and profit needs (sometimes, but not always equally, understandable).

Microorganisms with Emerging Antibiotic Resistances

Today, we have a dozen or so good antibiotics, but there's also significant antibiotic resistance capabilities in the bacterial populations of infections and infectious diseases we must treat. Why are these resistant microorganisms such a problem?

Sometime in the late 1950s, Japanese microbiologists noticed that penicillin was no longer as effective in dealing with bacterial infections as it had been. They began to look at various patients in a few selected hospitals to determine the frequency with which resistant organisms appeared in the total population of different isolated organisms. During a five-year period, starting around 1955, these microbiologists saw the relative number of resistant organisms had increased. These resistant organisms were able to destroy penicillin before it ever got close. The newly resistant bacteria had produced a protein—an enzyme that hydrolyzed the penicillin. Using a water molecule to help with the reaction, the enzyme cut penicillin molecules into two pieces (hence the term *hydrolyze*, in which *hydro* refers to water and *lyze* to splitting).

Where did this enzyme come from? The bacterial cells that were somehow resistant to the penicillin molecules had learned to make it. What was interesting was that the discovery was once again related to a new function, presumably carried out by a new enzyme. Nothing was known about this enzyme. We would not have recognized it if it had somehow appeared in our laboratories, perhaps packed in a little bottle. (Many known enzymes are packed in little bottles that one can buy from small companies making enzyme preparations.)

The only thing the scientific community did know was that "it" did something to penicillin. A lot remained to be learned. When these new enzyme-making bacteria encountered other bacteria that did not make the enzyme, this capability could be acquired from the resistant bacteria. This was very interesting. The presumably simple little bacteria, so small that a trillion of them could be packed in the space occupied by your finger tip, knew how to teach one another an important survival function. In this case, the lesson was how to survive in the presence of an otherwise lethal antibiotic.

A lot of people in Japan, Europe, and the US began to study this phenomenon. It soon became clear that resistant bacteria carried little extra pieces of DNA that were distinct from the larger DNA molecule (later called the *genome*), which contained all the information (genes) necessary to build and maintain a fully functional bacterium. These little chunks of non-genomic DNA contained the required information for bacteria to make the new enzyme that disabled penicillin. One might imagine that the bacteria had a large hard disk with information as well as little USB sticks with files about how to build themselves that were then passed around. They used the USB sticks to share the trick they'd learned (namely, how to make the resistant enzyme, which became known as penicillinase). So, long before we ever thought of USB sticks, bacteria had developed a system to transfer information needed to build this and other essential enzymes among the population. Teaching *avant la lettre* . . .

A fungus tries to defend itself and its territory against encroaching bacteria, so it sends out something that damages bacteria and ultimately causes them to fall apart (to "lyse"). But sooner or later, that defensive fungus comes up against bacteria that have learned to destroy the fungal protective compound before it gets to them. This begins to look like the escalation of military defenses to destroy attacking missiles in the stratosphere before attackers ever reach their targets.

By the early 1960s, the basis of antibiotic resistance was becoming clear. At some time in the not too distant future, most bacteria cultured from infected patients would be resistant to penicillin. Doctors realized they would not be able to use penicillin forever, so a search for other antibiotics was already underway. New discoveries and pathogens made it more urgent to have different antibiotics, antibiotics that had not yet triggered the development of resistance and were available to fight bacterial infections.

The bacteria proved as clever as we were, and they were rapidly evolving. By 1970, several species of multidrug resistant bacteria began to emerge; they now had developed resistance to several antibiotics. A race was on, with industrial and academic efforts to find new antibiotics while the bacterial pathogens equipped themselves for counter-attacks. Who would ultimately win this battle?

Forty years later, it does not look like we humans will be the winners. One problem is that we have only a limited number of bacterial functions to attack in an effort to kill or inactivate pathogenic bacteria. Why? We have too much in common. Our metabolisms are similar. We both use the same amino acids to make proteins, the same sugars to make polysaccharides, the same nucleotides to make DNA and RNA, and rather similar lipids to make our cell membranes. If we discover or develop chemical compounds that block or damage a particular bacterial process (say, the utilization of glucose), then this compound is very likely to do these same thing to our own glucose utilization. So we end up looking for things that bacteria must do and that we do not.

One major difference is that bacteria live as single cells. They have a cell wall structure that looks something like an outer layer of chicken wire wrapped around a pliable, fragile membrane. This inner membrane keeps some important molecules from leaking out of the cell and other molecules from getting in willy-nilly.

Our cells, which join together to form tissues, don't have the same type of walls. So, attacking bacteria's cell wall structure is a useful approach. In fact, this is where the first identified antibiotic, penicillin, acts. Penicillin prevents bacterial cells from building proper walls. The bacteria do, however, continue to grow. Sooner or later, the weakened inner membrane that is supposed to keep everything together ruptures and the cell basically disintegrates (or undergoes hydrolysis—that same term again). When the cell wall ruptures, the cell is torn open, its contents leak out, and the cell ceases to be a clearly defined single structure. End of bacterium.

• • •

A little more about bacteria. If one adds a colored compound to various kinds of bacteria and then attempts to wash away the color with water, some bacteria will lose the color and others will not.

What exactly is happening? That was not clear back in 1884, when Hans Christian Gram, a German microbiologist, first did this simple experiment. The researcher picks up some bacteria from a plated culture with a toothpick, swirls the toothpick around in a droplet of water, places a droplet on a small glass microscope slide, and then lets the water evaporate. The bacterial cells dry out and stick to the glass. The staining solution, a liquid that contains a colored compound, is then added onto the slide. The colored molecules adhere to the cells either tightly or not so tightly. When the stained cells are rinsed with water or alcohol, the stain either comes off or stays on. If the stain comes off easily, it was not very tightly bound to the cells. The staining depends on the kind of bacteria.

The procedure is now named after Gram. Today, researchers still do Gram staining. Bacteria are called Gram-positive (they keep the color) or Gram-negative (they lose the color).

The question of why this happens was answered around 1940. It turned out that Gram-positive bacteria have very thick cell walls. Gram-negative cells are different. They are surrounded by a thin layer that provides some structural strength but much less than the structural strength supplied by Gram-positive walls. However (and this seems to be a key difference), Gram-negative bacteria have a second membrane structure around the thin hard wall. This makes for a wall structure something like cardboard, where two thin paper layers are separated by a corrugated layer and the three together form a very light but relatively strong flat sheet. In contrast, the envelope around the Gram-positives is more like a plank of wood.

...

What Makes an Antibiotic Suitable?

Various antibiotics that interfere with different organisms' wall synthesis have been developed. These generally do not affect metabolic or cellular processes in humans and animals, and therefore, they have been useful. Many of these are variants of penicillin, including penicillin G, cephalosporin, and daptomycin—a recent addition.

Gram-negative bacteria produce various molecules that end up in the outer membrane. There are protein molecules and various polysaccharides that are part of this outer membrane; some of these have also become targets for antibiotics. Others may still be found.

In contrast to their cell walls, bacteria and animal cells build their proteins using similar general approaches. However, some parts of the machinery differ. This means that some antibiotics used against bacteria can potentially block or damage protein synthesis without affecting the processes of an infected animal's host cells. The antibiotics chloramphenicol and streptomycin work this way.

RNA synthesis is not completely identical in animals and bacteria. Though closely related, there are differences in the details. Antibiotics such as rifampicin and rifamycin, which block bacterial RNA synthesis, exploit these differences, thereby preventing growth and division of the bacterial cells.[28]

---

28   Rifampicin is a semisynthetic antibiotic produced from *Streptomyces mediterranei*.
     Rifamycin is a natural antibiotic produced by *Streptomyces mediterranei* (ansamycin family).

Bacteria have evolved methods to deal with each of these compounds. Some bacteria are even able to handle many antibiotics simultaneously, and these bacteria then pose larger threats. One can imagine a time when there are no longer effective antibiotics for new organisms appearing in our environment.

Although academic and industrial groups continue looking for new and variant antibiotics, the search has become a game of diminishing returns. Because we are limited to bacterial targets that are clearly different from our own cell's related targets, we're limited. As a result, the best targets have, over the last fifty years, been addressed with considerable success. Finding additional antibiotics with new targets has become progressively more difficult. Not impossible, but difficult.

Another rather interesting difficulty is that it's unlikely that a good antibiotic may be a very profitable product for the pharmaceutical industry. The better the antibiotic, the more physicians will want to hold it in reserve for emergencies. So, ideally, it will not be widely used.

An ideal pharmaceutical compound is one that works better than whatever else is on the market and should be taken daily for the rest of the patient's life. My flecainide is such a compound. I have not figured out how to live without it. Since I do not yet see any side effects, this is fine. In addition, flecainide is relatively inexpensive and my insurance takes care of most of the cost, so even that does not particularly concern me.

Many other drugs are used daily and at considerably higher cost to the consumer or insurance company. The insurer, of course, has to recover costs, pay for its organization, and make a reasonable profit for shareholders. One way or another, insurers will have to set monthly rates to cover such costs.

The same is true of an ICD, which is considerably more costly than a drug like flecainide. At a cost of CHF 12,000 (Swiss francs) per year, an ICD is a recurring item that, in theory, users will have to pay for for the rest of their lives. Users pay directly or via the insurance system. As a patient participating in the Swiss insurance system, this has not worried me too much. As the writer of this book, it does concern me. Sooner or later, these costs have to be absorbed by someone.

At any rate, from a commercial point of view, antibiotics are not particularly attractive development targets. However, with the emergence of multidrug resistant bacteria, there is an urgent need to develop alternative drugs. This is a problem that is now widely discussed, not only in the scientific press but also in various newspapers, magazines, and television shows.

• • •

Do you remember encountering any teachers who would occasionally go "off script" in a lecture? They brought such enthusiasm to their subject that excluding any details of who did what and how that experiment was actually done would just be impossible.

This essay is that kind of lecture. Bernie had dedicated his professional life to these subjects. His worldview unified the ecology of microorganisms with how hospitals function; antibiotics made sense because he understood how and why they worked. Resistance to antibiotics could be overcome with more rational use of the drugs.

He wants to tell you so much! You really must know how an agar plate is made, how Fleming found penicillin, how Gram stained his slides, and how a cow digests grass. These things are all equally exciting. How could he possibly leave something out when it was so pressing, so important, to tell his students and readers everything?

CHAPTER 22

Playing with All of the Pills

Bernie called it "playing with the pills"; I call it "self-experimentation."
No matter what you call it, as a doctor, I don't recommend it. Over
the years, my friendship with Bernie taught me the importance of self-
restraint. If he didn't ask, he didn't want my opinion, and I didn't offer it.

• • •

Two months on, my energy level was higher. I spent April measuring my blood pressure and heart rate and playing with all of
the pills I had been given to deal with high blood pressure. I made
about six hundred blood pressure and heart rate measurements.
This useful data showed that the standard deviations from average blood pressure values amounted to about 12 percent. On the
whole, average blood pressure dropped to about 140/80; without
any pills (lisinopril, aka. Zestril) and aside from the standard 100
mg flecainide and 25 mg metoprolol succinate every morning,
that reading increased to 155/95 and higher. So, some lisinopril
might not be a bad idea. Aldactone and aspirin might also have
been useful, but I only used lisinopril in addition to flecainide and
metoprolol succinate during the weeks when my blood pressure
decreased to 140/80.

I spent a lot of energy on measuring blood pressure and heart rate in April, but having seen improvements, I stopped measuring in May 2008. Since then, I have limited myself to my daily flecainide (100 mg) and metoprolol succinate (25 mg) dosage.

When, if I recall correctly, Prof. Rolf Jenni found my EF to be 45%, I also stopped thinking about measurements. I did a little rowing on the machine, but because of maintenance on our apartment exterior, I moved my Concept2 to the basement at the end of May and have only touched a rowing machine at The Red Lion Inn from July 8 through 12.[29]

When the scaffolding around our apartment is removed in the next few days, the Concept2 will come back up, and I can begin to rebuild a little more fitness, rowing perhaps three times per week.

Incidentally, Renske is about to start a new project in Den Haag (The Hague), and we looked for an apartment this past weekend (July 25, 2008). The likely selection will be a Vesteda apartment above Centraal Station in Den Haag; its gym boasts a Concept2. So, three rowing sessions per week, at the end of the day, are possible.

I have also agreed with Prof. Karrer, the infectious disease consultant, that I will meet Prof. Duru, the heart rhythm specialist, to conclude the experimental phase and determine how I shall proceed now that I no longer have an ICD to protect me if and when I get hit with a tachycardia.

Beyond that, I should have another echocardiogram towards the end of the year to see where my EF is. It would not be a bad

---

29   Not to be confused with the chain of hotels, The Red Lion Inn is an historic hotel in Stockbridge, Massachusetts.

idea to look into the blood flow modeling in constricted arteries, something I promised to do for Prof. Jenni after the last examination on April 28, 2008, three months ago.

• • •

As 2008 moved along, and after the upheaval with the ICD-related infection, which was followed by the debate about proper technique for the infected device's removal, Bernie's life had returned more or less to normal: looking for an apartment in The Hague, paying attention to Renske's career, and trying, once again, to get back to rowing.

In other words, he turned to the coping strategies that had worked for him before.

CHAPTER 23

Back to Rowing: No ICD

Into summer 2009.

...

I had meantime started my various exercise routines, including rowing stretches on my Concept2 with the various heart rate and power measurements I had started using in 2003. It was nice to be back on the machine and begin to feel my body again. It did not take long for my heart to begin behaving as I had previously experienced. It was a little messy initially, but after a few kilometers on the rowing machine, my heart fell into line and the regulation of my heart rate was as I had seen it since 2004.

One day, after having left the hospital and using the Concept2 machine for routine exercises, I felt I was ready for some rowing with my Grasshopper Club friends. I had programmed the desired heart rate range on my Polar watch between 50 and 160 bpm and had also set the monitor to produce the usual beeps when my heart rate was outside this range.

The first thing to do prior to rowing is to take the boat out of the boathouse, set it on stretchers on the lawn, adjust the footboard, check the state of and make adjustments to the outriggers and oarlocks, and see that the seat runs nicely on its tracks; in general, make sure everything is in good order. Then, the boat is carried to the dock and lowered into the water; oars are placed in the oarlocks and the locks properly closed; and a water bottle is placed somewhere near one's seat. At that point, it is time to get into the boat and shove off. And so we did that sunny morning in mid-2009.

This entire procedure felt less than great. Although the boat did not weigh that much, getting started involved carrying it from the boathouse, where it had to be pulled out of its supports, hoisted on the shoulders, slowly moved past various obstacles, and turned over before placing it in the stretchers outside. After making the adjustments, we once again picked up the boat, first lifting it from the stretchers and overhead before placing the boat onto our shoulders. Then we proceeded to walk it down a slippery ramp onto an equally slippery dock, where the boat was once again turned, this time at the edge of the floating dock, which bobbed up and down, and lowered down onto the water. All of this activity always included moments where a lot more than the average weight was on just a few shoulders or arms—often, so it felt, on mine. This was my classical tachycardia territory: no warm-up, sudden efforts, now and then exertion, and now what . . .

That first time, while walking the boat down the ramp, I picked up the sound of that little *beep . . . beep . . . beep . . .* Oh, shit!

By the time my arms were free and I was able to look— maybe thirty seconds later—my Polar watch displayed a perfectly fine 95 bpm. OK, that was just a blip.

I stepped into the four, pushed off, sat down, and rowed a few strokes to get clear of the dock. Then we settled in, tying our shoes, riding up and down the tracks, breathing that lake-y wet

air, and generally being happy to be sitting there. Almost acciden-
tally, I glanced at my watch and saw 240 bpm looking back at me.
I just kept staring. We were not yet moving. Discouraging,
quite. Do I tell my mates I need to get back and get out of the
boat? Do I stay? "What the hell," I heard myself saying. "Let's just
see what happens."

Within a few strokes, the 240 reading was gone. It was a nice
row, for the usual twelve or fifteen kilometers. This first row since
the ETH Zurich "Professoren" race in November 2007 was marvelous, and more were to follow.

Short bursts of tachycardia were not uncommon. They typically lasted ten to thirty seconds and never more than one or
two minutes. I rarely felt anything when my monitor sensed one
of the ten- to thirty-second bursts. The longer bursts, those one-
to two-minutes episodes, I did sometimes sense; the feeling was
something like a hiccup in my chest, as though my heart were
skipping one or two beats and then racing to once again catch its
normal rhythm.

I noticed that, after that short tachycardia experienced on my
first post-ICD rowing outing, I would see similar events with
some regularity. I saw these only when I wore my Polar chest
belt and heart rate monitor combination; I wore the Polar devices
when I rowed on the Concept2, when I biked, and on various
other occasions for one reason or another.

I heard enough blips in the following weeks that, at one point,
I turned off the beeping. I rarely saw a heart rate I did not like,
but I had, of course, hidden part of the data. Not very scientific,
but I was now moving into year ten of these experiments, and
sometimes, I'd get a little tired of all that information.

I considered that these bursts might come from extraneous

sources. This was certainly the case when I was near tram or train tracks or when I walked or biked under high power lines.

I also experienced much more instability when I biked in and around Zurich, especially when I was straining to go up a hill. I did not understand what exactly was going on here. One possibility was that various veins in my legs were squeezed as my thighs moved past and pressed against the narrow racing saddle. Another possibility was that my heart bounced around more during biking than in a boat or on the Concept2 rowing machine.

I had seen this between 1999 and 2006, when I still jogged regularly. Going down a hill often triggered a tachycardia, which resulted from the deeper drop as my forward foot hit the ground. Evidently my heart's physical jarring within my chest affected the heart rate regulation system in some way.

By mid-2008, I still saw occasional tachycardia, perhaps one or two for every three or five sessions I'd wear the Polar monitor. When I did wear it, I probably had it on for three or four hours, during and after rowing, walking, or working out on the Concept2 machine. A very rough estimate of the number of these short-lived tachycardia, typically less than thirty seconds long, would be one per three sessions, or one per ten to twelve hours, equal to perhaps two per day. At 200 to 240 bpm for these short tachycardia, each might consist of around 50 to 150 beats, or perhaps 100 to 300 closely spaced beats per day.

Was this more than I had seen when I still had an ICD? The major trigger-happy period for the device, when I received a number of shocks, was January 2000, shortly after implantation. Later, the device was rarely triggered (only twice since 2002 and probably not at all after 2006).

It seems reasonable to conclude that, while there had been

continued bursts of fewer than one hundred beats, I experienced very few sustained tachycardia after I started taking flecainide in 2001. This was true for the eight years before and the five years after my ICD was removed.

• • •

Was it stubborn for Bernie to continue with that row? Perhaps foolhardy? Yes to both questions.

But for Bernie, it was very simple. Over the years with his illness, Bernie had realized that, if he could not live the life he wanted, then he didn't care that much about life itself. He had learned to savor the moments of joy in his daily life, and he wasn't willing to give them up just to have more uneventful days.

In the short section that follows, Bernie expresses his existential core more directly.

• • •

Like the old days in São Paulo when I was an eight-, nine-, and ten-year-old just in from sweet Holland, I have had to face and do things that I most certainly would have preferred not to face or do.

Even though the flecainide began working its magic for me after those first fifteen or sixteen months, and despite everything I had learned about tachycardia and various drugs, it took me more than four years before I thought of sitting on a rowing machine. I had to look at what my heart did when I made various modest efforts and gradually learn to continue looking even when I definitely did not like what I saw.

Had there been help back in São Paulo, I would have run for

it. My younger brothers? Pa? They listened, said little. I understood, even then.

Ma? Sometimes she sat in a window, sobbing, threatening to jump out. I remember her beauty, her tears, her flowery dress fluttering in the wind around her bare legs and shoeless feet—and knowing a one-story plunge would not kill her, I shrugged.

No help, though. Back then in São Palo, it was just me and my little strategies. And now, half a century later? Still just me and my slightly bigger strategies. That's what we have—mostly, how it's always been. So, Brazil, thanks for the lessons so well taught.

CHAPTER 24

Diet and Exercise

Sometime in late 2009, we had Werner and Gabriela Kieser over for dinner.

Werner presented us with a book he had recently written about his approaches to muscle building. He had set up a chain of some 150 power-building centers around Europe and Australia, based on an approach he had begun developing in the 1960s. The general idea was to build the central core musculature, thereby stiffening the torso into a solid core structure for the legs, shoulders, and neck. I had known about his thinking and sport centers but had never thought about his approach. I was happy with my rowing and Concept2 machine and did not spend any time on other options.

After reading his book, I realized there was more that could be done to strengthen myself and signed up. Werner was convinced that all the color, sounds, and general happiness seen in many commercial gyms was distracting. His shops were various shades of grey; there was a water fountain and very little banter or talking. I did my routine as advised, and I did gain strength in my back and limbs. The workouts did not harm my rowing. I began looking a little at other approaches and started thinking a little about diets.

The latter point—diets—had always seemed rather useless to

me. After all, I was a biochemist. I taught students how various molecules were transformed into the essential building blocks to produce all that our cells need to function. I knew all about the sugars, amino acids, bases, fats, lipids, vitamins, metals, trace minerals; what more did we need to know?

A few months after we started frequenting one of Werner's gyms, my wife and I had dinner with some of my Amherst friends near New York. After that, we spent a weekend with Roger and Katherine Mills in New Jersey. [*We had made a corporate move from the San Francisco Bay area to New Jersey in 2008.*] We had our usual fine conversations about politics, health, and life, and I did a little rowing on Roger's rowing machine. We also touched on nutrition and developing musculature. On Monday before we left, we stopped at a shopping mall where the ladies had business. I wandered through the local bookstore, found the health section, and was soon busy selecting the best sports nutrition books I could find.

• • •

Yes, Bernie rowed on my Concept2. I could not watch. I sat upstairs in the kitchen and listened carefully so that I would hear the machine stop and his body hit the floor. I had a plan to resuscitate him and call 911. Nothing happened. Was I aiding and abetting?

• • •

I found two books. *Men's Health Power Training* by Robert dos Remedios and *The US Navy SEAL Guide to Fitness and Nutrition* turned out to be very interesting and useful. I discovered that these were excellent complements to what we teach in biochemistry, coupling the biochemistry to physical performance. Both books see the body as a machine, the performance of which can be modulated and optimized, which is how I also like to think of this body of ours.

Robert dos Remedios has helped all sorts of athletes develop more power, which they have then used to improve their specific sport disciplines. Every statement in his book made sense to me. No hype, no great promises. If you understand how the machine works, you can fuel it a little better, train it better, and take it further in whatever direction you wish.

The production and utilization of glycogen was such a topic. I knew all about the biochemistry of glycogen (or more precisely, of starch), having worked on this for six or seven years. However, I had never thought much about diurnal cycles of its synthesis and utilization, though this is very basic and common knowledge among nutritionists and trainers. So here I was, a specialist seeing various trees but missing the forest, much like my heart specialists. Some look at the heart and see every little structural detail, while others look at function and see totally different things. This cannot be helped; the complexity is so great that we can only really understand a few components or aspects in detail.

At any rate, glycogen, like starch, is a chain of glucose molecules that are linked together to become one of these two biopolymers, both polysaccharides. All these words describe the same material but stress different properties of these molecules. *Biopolymers* refers to polymers of biomolecules. *Polymers* can be broken down to *poly* (many) and *monomers* (only a single unit), with the many monomers linked to form the polymers. *Polysaccharides* specifies the sort of monomer molecules in the polymer, namely saccharides or sugars; in this case, glucose is a *monosaccharide,* meaning that it is a single sugar ring or molecule. There exist *disaccharides*, or two rings, two identical or different monomers. There are also *tri-*, *tetra-*, and *pentasaccharides*. At some point we say *oligo-*, meaning a small number, and when that seems too few, we then move to *polysaccharides*. These may contain thousands or tens of thousands of monomers.

So when we eat a slice of bread, it will contain starch from wheat, barley, or corn. This will be broken down in the stomach into smaller particles. In the intestine, the starch is depolymerized, meaning that various enzymes will cut off glucose at the end of each polymer chain. This process will continue until the entire chain has been converted to individual glucose molecules.

These will be taken up by the cells lining the gut. Individual glucose molecules (or short oligomers) will then be transported to the blood and carried around the body. At some point, these glucose molecules will be taken up by our cells—among them, our muscle cells. These will either utilize the glucose by converting it into smaller molecules or the glucose will again be polymerized and form a molecule very similar, if not identical, to starch. When made in our bodies, this molecule is called *glycogen*.

Why does a cell first take up the glucose and then synthesize a polymer rather than just storing the glucose as is? One answer is that a lot of small molecules behave differently from a single chain made up of many of the same small molecules. Imagine storing ten thousand beads in a drawer full of other things versus having all those beads on a single string or a little tree-like structure.

Muscle cells can contain enough glycogen to work for a half hour, more or less. After this intracellular energy source has been depleted, our cells have to start working with glucose or fats imported from blood. This requires a little more effort from the system. (As an aside, the cell also has a small supply of energy in the form of creatine phosphate and adenosine triphosphate, or ATP, molecules that release their energy almost instantly. This supply is good for about thirty seconds and comes in handy when you have to jump out of the way of on oncoming car.)

When you sleep, your cells continue working. You breathe, blood circulates, your brain may be busy, and a certain amount of maintenance goes on. Some of the energy for this work comes from glycogen stored in muscle cells. As a result, glycogen supplies are low early in the morning. Taking in some readily available fuel molecules to rebuild glycogen supplies is a good idea. This, as Dos Remedios reminded me, is why athletes take in carbohydrates—either as solids or liquids—in the morning and start their workouts at least a half hour after ingesting.

As workouts proceed, endurance athletes need to take in more fuel. They can utilize glycogen stored in the liver, but the better supplies are fats and lipids stored within muscles, under the skin, and in various fairly specific fat stores around the waist, arms, and legs.

A workout generally entails a certain amount of wear and tear on muscles, tendons, and bone cartilage, which consist of various macromolecules; proteins are the major component, so that after a workout there will be synthesis of new protein molecules. This means there must be an adequate supply of amino acids, protein's building blocks. Ten of the twenty amino acids used for the synthesis of new proteins are not produced ourselves. These must, therefore, be provided in our diets. They can be presented as whole proteins in meat, poultry, fish, or plants. We eat these foods and break down proteins; the amino acids make it into our blood stream via the small intestine.

Interesting things happen at this stage. We use the twenty amino acids in different amounts because each protein molecule produced by our cells contains varying amounts of these different amino acids. If we obtain too much of a particular amino acid, it will have to be broken down. This results in the accumulation of amino-rich waste molecules, usually in the form of urea in our cells. Our kidneys get rid of this excess, which ends up in urine. Sometimes, this system does not work all that well and some of the urea crystallizes out. Crystals are lumps of accumulated molecules that do not dissolve in the water in our cells. These molecules stick together to form ordered packets of molecules. These crystals can be hard packets with sharp edges and can no longer leave our body via the bladder. Instead, they might accumulate somewhere in organs or tissues where they are no longer able to leave (like toes or the scrotum). This is chemistry at work, doing what can be seen in the laboratory. Very painful when it happens in a body.

The solution? Do not ingest more poorly soluble amino acids than are needed to produce new proteins.

• • •

Well, there's some practical advice. Needless to say, I did not share Bernie's enthusiasm on the topic.

• • •

On the other hand, as repair is necessary after workouts, it's important to ingest enough to produce proteins as needed. The nutritionists have worked out the ideal amounts of various proteins to be taken in, which is where *The Navy SEAL Guide* provides interesting and useful information.

Navy SEALs are trained to deal with a variety of difficult tasks that require excellent condition and endurance. The amount of fuel required to carry out various tasks (such as hiking ten miles with fifty pounds of equipment over soggy terrain and elevation changes of five hundred feet, at temperatures between freezing and very hot) can be predicted and has been validated. The same is true for a one-mile swim in cold water against winds and waves, again with a significant amount of equipment.

The lessons learned from observing these young bodies under extreme conditions are useful for all of us, in the same way that performance improvements in Formula One racing leads to improvements of standard cars.

Important for Navy SEALs are not only their training and adequate fuel and repair compound resources but also how much of these their bodies store. They are highly trained, but unlike Tour de France cyclists, the goal is not to carry as little fuel as possible. The opposite might be more applicable: Carry enough reserves to survive a few days without refueling.

• • •

It was absolutely impossible for Bernie to talk about nutrition without somehow involving the Tour de France. I would just listen and nod; his enthusiasm for the topic was sufficient to sustain the conversation.

• • •

So, being in good shape and looking lithe are not necessarily the same thing. I would prefer to be in good shape—my body capable of doing what I want it to do—and looking a bit heavier than my wife would like me to look rather than the opposite (looking good, according to my wife, but in so-so condition). Fortunately, once I get in shape, it is rather easy to eat less.

How careful do we need to be about what we eat? Not very. We take in sugars, mostly as starch, which will be broken down to glucose and utilized directly or stored in glycogen in the liver and muscles. There is no penalty for eating sugar as such, either in coffee, tea, or various drinks, as long as our body uses it for work. We also take in fats in many forms: in meat, milk, yogurt, butter, cheese, ice cream, cookies, cakes, nuts, and various plants. As long as we burn these foods, there is no problem. If we accumulate some, this will be used when we eat a little less or use our bodies a little more.

Up until springtime 2010, I had always eaten a lot of ice cream (probably a half liter most days for the previous fifty years). I never thought much about what I ate, secure in the knowledge that most foodstuffs are interchangeable. Vegetables and fruits are fine for some of the vitamins, but I tended to regard veggies mostly as organized water.

After reading *The Navy SEAL Guide* and Dos Remedios's book, I stopped eating ice cream, cut out most cheese, and saw my weight coming back to what it was in 1992 when all was well and I had last rowed the Amsterdam Head of the River races (7.5 km in both eights and a single scull). I went from the 92–93 kilos (about 202 lbs.) I had been at for the previous fifteen years to 85–86 (about 188 lbs.) in a few weeks. It was quite painless.

Suddenly ice cream and cheese were not as tasty as they had been, and it was pleasant to walk around with seven fewer kilos to carry around. In 2011, I joined the ETH Zurich "Professoren" eight once again. The early morning rows were easier with the prior glycogen buildup and lots of water, as advised by the two guidebooks. The race was harder than in 2006 or even 2007, and we lost to the University of Zurich. However, everything worked well enough. I had heart rates above 160 bpm at the end of the races but no tachycardia.

I found the following simple basics sufficient: Get enough sleep; injest vitamins as fruits and fresh vegetables; eat meat and bread as desired; have whatever else tastes good, including coffee, wine, and an occasional cigar; and most importantly, no more calories in than go out for daily life and workouts of some sort. No big news here; this is all general knowledge.

• • •

We had a wonderful visit with Bernie and Renske. We were living in a rented house on a horse farm in Whitehouse Station, New Jersey, and the four of us enjoyed lunch together in Lambertville.

After Bernie started his more intensive diet and exercise program, he seemed fully recovered from his bout with infection. He was confident that he could get back to rowing without the ICD as backup.

I had mixed emotions, one of which was certainly jealousy. After years of rowing, skiing, and tennis, I had both hips replaced in the late 1990s. After the surgery, I returned to rowing on my own Concept2. Eventually, this led to having the left hip operated on again after twelve years. My rowing career was over; he had joined his professors' eight again.

On the other hand, his heart problems had never been fully diagnosed or treated. The two of us were steadily getting older. "Better lucky than smart" has always been as true in medicine as in any other discipline. Had Bernie just been lucky so far?

CHAPTER 25

Back to the ETH Boat

2012.

• • •

Rowing with my ETH Zurich friends was going to be more demanding than the Grasshopper Club rows, since our season would end in a best of three 600 meter sprints regatta against the University of Zurich professors. We had done well enough from 2004 to 2007.

I did not feel it wise to join this boat in 2008, nor did my family or Prof. Duru, my cardiologist. This was also true in 2009 and 2010.

By 2011, several professors had decided not to continue rowing. I was asked to be available just in case. I joined my friends. We lost.

Clearly, more work had to be done if we were to do better in 2012.

Since 2008, I had focused on 10 km endurance rows on the Concept2 machine. I typically started out with an easy 1 km warm-up stretch, then a one minute rest, followed by a second somewhat harder 1 km stretch and one minute rest, and then the

10 km stretch at a constant speed, which ended at a heart rate of around 160 bpm. This was finally followed by an easy cool down.

My best time for the 10 km length averaged two minutes and seven seconds per 500 meter split sustained over the entire distance. This was equal to my time from 2005 (after the second ICD) and before my knee arthroscopy and ICD infection in 2007.[30]

In subsequent years, I generally started training periods with my average 10 km times around two minutes and twenty-five seconds per 500 meters. I managed to bring this time down to two minutes and fifteen seconds or two minutes and twelve seconds after a few weeks. I was happy enough with these results for 2011 but wanted to do better for 2012.

How good or bad were these times? How might tachycardia and an EF of around 45% affect my performance compared to men my age with normal heart regulation? I have always been interested in seeing what times I can reasonably target for 500 meters as I age.

• • •

I used the website Bernie discusses next when I was rowing on my own Concept2. The site shows where each rower ranks among age-group peers. The numbers Bernie achieved with his own "safe" approach would've put him in the top ten percent of his age group. That relative scale was not enough for Bernie.

• • •

---

30   This is the only time I'm aware of that Bernie acknowledged the relationship of his arthroscopy and his ICD infection.

The Concept2 website has a feature that keeps track of times sent in by rowers (men and women, heavyweight or lightweight) for various distances (500 meters and 1, 2, 5, and 10 km, as well as half and full marathons and 100 km). I have downloaded the 2011 data for heavyweight men and for several distances.

I plotted the times versus age and determined average times for each decade of age (ages one through ten, eleven through twenty, twenty-one through thirty, and on up to eighty-one through ninety) and, to the extent available, added numbers for my ETH Zurich colleagues to see how we shaped up in comparison to our rowing confreres worldwide.

When all 2,654 men who provided 500 meter data to the Concept2 site in 2011 are included, we see a fair number of young boys ages six to ten years old and a smattering of men from twenty-five to eighty-six with times between two minutes and thirty seconds to four minutes. The average time for 500 meters for successive decades is fairly constant up to the fifth decade, after which it increases steadily and rapidly as men age.

To focus on the highly motivated set of rowers, I produced a second plot, where I eliminated 207 rowers with times longer than two minutes for 500 meters. This skewed the data, cutting off increasing numbers of rowers as their ages increased, since completing 500 meters in two minutes is harder at age eighty than at age thirty. Still, this plot looked useful. The average times for 500 meters by decade are nearly constant up to the fifth decade (forty to fifty). The changes in the sixth to eighth decades remain fairly constant and are still moderate. Amazingly, average 500 meter times for all these men increased by only nine seconds from the group in their thirties (one minute and thirty-seven seconds) to those in their sixties (one minute and forty-six seconds). The number of rowers in their seventies who submit 500 meter data is small: just fifty-two

(averaging two minutes) for the entire data set and thirty-four
(averaging one minute and fifty-one seconds) for the limited set
(eighteen were eliminated for times greater than two minutes). Still,
it is apparently possible to keep doing 500 meter sprints in only five
more seconds as one ages from one's sixties to seventies.

Finally, if we focus on this more motivated sub-two-minute
group of men, their average age-based performance overlapped
surprisingly well with our ETH Zurich "Professoren" trend line.
[*I do not have the plots, but I believe the data.*]

So, we are sort of motivated and sort of average, doing about
as well as the more active general Concept2 user set. Knocking
five or maybe eight seconds off our present times does not look
that forbidding . . .

. . .

*I don't agree with this interpretation. The group of seventy-year-old men
recording 500 meter times of under two minutes on the Concept2 website
represents extreme outliers. These are very fit individuals. It's like saying,
"I was just your average Phi Beta Kappa frat boy."*

Heart Rate Behavior Following
a Short Burst of Effort

Given our short sprints, I began to focus on shorter higher-power
stretches, and I began to try to reduce my time for a single 500
meter stretch followed by two series of nine short runs varying
from 150 to 250 meters, each followed by two-minute rests.

Doing these workouts every other day, in addition to time
on the water, I gradually reduced my 500 meter times by a few

tenths of seconds per session, from 1:47.5 to 1:45.2. This was in the range also obtained by my younger friends in the boat. I felt fine with these results.

Still, not all was perfect.

My heart rate pattern during these short rowing bursts, which began around 350 watts in intensity and ended around 300 watts, differed from the 10 km long stretches at around 150 watts not only during the power burst but during the recovery phase at the end of the burst as well.

With the short power stretches, my heart rate increased very nicely from an initial rate around 100 bpm to 155 or 160 bpm at the end of a 500 meter stretch or to 140 bpm at the end of a 200 meter stretch; these numbers were totally understandable. At the end of the burst, when the two-minute recovery started, my heart rate decreased in an orderly and reproducible manner for about a minute and a half, declining from about 155 to 130 bpm after a 500 meter burst and from 140 to 120 bpm after a 200 meter burst.

Then my heart rate became unstable. Sometimes it continued decreasing and then increased again after five or ten seconds; sometimes it might stop decreasing, then increase, decrease, and so on, or it might begin to increase immediately after those first ninety seconds of an orderly decrease.

If I then started off with another 200 or 250 meter burst, my heart rate would almost always restart at the same level, usually around 100 to 110 bpm, regardless of where it had been at the end of the chaotic rest period.

A different, rather interesting observation was that when I took a five-minute rest after a series of nine short (150 to 250 meter) bursts, it seemed as though my heart anticipated a tenth burst, with my heart rate increasing as though I were actually rowing when I was, in fact, only resting. This looked like some sort of memory effect, with my heart mumbling, "OK, mate, you have done nine of these bursts. How am I supposed to know there will *not* be a tenth?"

I did not understand these phenomena at the time, although the observations seemed to add a little information to the discussion about neural (central) versus hormonal signaling.

More to the point, by July and August 2012, I realized that I was entering unknown territory. I decided I should return to endurance rows, perhaps interspersing one 10 km row for every two or three power exercises. Continuously alternating the two types of exercises would possibly be even better.

Any coach would probably have told me this.

• • •

I suspect that, if queried, almost any coach would have told a seventy-one-year-old man with well-documented recurrent ventricular tachycardia to get the hell out of the boat! But Bernie knew well enough not to ask questions when he did not want to hear the answers.

From an objective point of view, Bernie either did not realize or consciously denied that he had changed the conditions of his self-experimentation. When he began to explore his heart rate responses to exercise, he had the fail-safe protection of his ICD as well as the less-complete moderating effects of his two antiarrhythmic drugs. He had learned that he did best with warm-up sessions before heavy exertion, and pacing himself with endurance exercise resulted in fewer problems than short maximum-effort sprints. By "doing the same experiment over and over again," he had achieved considerable success.

In 2012, without the backing of an ICD, he set out on a course of completely ignoring his years of prior disciplined self-study. His own data showed that he was heading for major problems as he prepared for the sprints. If he had been objective about the data, he would have said to his friends, "I don't think these sprint races are a good idea for me."

The heart rate responses that Bernie describes here suggest an imbalance in the systems that control increasing (sympathetic) and decreasing (parasympathetic) heart rate. Much of his previous story also supports this concept. It's impossible to know for a fact whether his short power rows made this more evident or whether his underlying disease was worsening. I suspect both factors played a part, but the change in exercise pattern seems key to me.

CHAPTER 26

The Zurich City Sprints

Our regatta was scheduled for September 29, 2012, and there was a new format for Zurich: the "City Sprints." The idea was to have spectators lined up along the Limmat River, which runs into the center of the city and is fed by Lake Zurich, which is in turn fed by alpine waters flowing from thirty kilometers to the east.

Top single scullers, double sculls, fours, and Olympic and national winners from various countries would show their stuff. Our ETH Zurich and University eights (including men's and women's eights and our "Professoren" boats) would row just one 400 meter sprint instead of the three 600 meter elimination sprints we had rowed in past years.

This new format required an all-or-nothing effort. It was all about having the best possible start for five strokes, followed by another ten strokes at about 38 strokes per minute in our boat. After that, we only had to row another thirty-five strokes at 34 or 36 strokes per minute to cover the entire 400 meters.[31]

I knew that training safely should include doing endurance

---

31 Intercollegiate and international races are usually 2000 meters. The boats cover this distance in about six minutes, allowing good crews at least a chance to make up for a slow start.

stretches. On the other hand, I also wanted to lower my 500 meter time for as much as possible, and I could not waste my training sessions on 10 km stretches. I felt that I just had to do more of the power workouts to see how far I could take this.

I told myself, "Explore the limits."

"Yes, sir," I answered.

My wife and I had decided to do some biking in Northern Italy, the South Tyrol—formerly part of the south of the Austro-Hungarian Empire and acquired by Italy at the end of the First World War. This seemed like a nice substitute for the endurance rows, which I would not do. We biked for three days through beautiful fruit and wine country, up and down gentle hills, all while getting plenty of exercise. My wife thought I looked worn out when we drove home.

Early the next morning, I prepared for one of our final 6:00 a.m. practice sessions in the eight. I felt strong. I took my trusted flecainide (although for the previous several weeks, I had cut the dose in half to 50 mg per day, given how well I was doing).

I had arrived at the boathouse a bit late. There was no time to do my standard 2 km warm-up at the boathouse. I had religiously done this preliminary exercise on the machines, knowing those first few kilometers were better not done in a boat with a crew that wanted to move fast right from the start.

Everything was under full control, and although I had brought my Polar belt and monitor, I saw no good reason to wear them.

We took off with a bit of a warm-up and then rowed on in a single 7 km stretch, ending with one of those marvelous 500 meter semi-sprints. I felt in control and good. Strong even. On top. The gods, however, were about to disagree.

CHAPTER 27

Letter from a Lucky Man

Thursday, September 13, 2012.

• • •

To Appie: [*Albert, one of Bernie's brothers*]

Rowing in Zurich: My boat will be there, but without me, though.

Absolutely, Ap, I would have been in that eight. Training for that was actually the cause of my near miss, or should I say, the Grim Reaper's near miss?

I started training pretty hard when we returned from Maine, and I kept at it by doing short power bursts: 500 meter stretches on the rowing machine at my maximum, whatever that might mean. Getting the time down from week to week (just by fractions of seconds . . .) by doing lots of 150, 200, and 250 meter stretches with one-and-a-half- or two-minute rests in between.

Each particular set of exercises has its own heart rate patterns. I started doing these measurements back in 2003 to understand what my heart was up to and to learn how to train my heart (if this is possible), rather than, or in addition to, training my legs, back, and so on.

The Concept2 rowing machine has a data-collection unit that measures stroke rate in strokes per minute, distance rowed as meters per stroke, and time to cover a given distance (x seconds to go 500 meters). My heart rate in beats per minute (bpm) is measured with a Polar chest strap and then sent to the data collector on the rowing machine. All of this information then goes into my computer, where I can watch it as I row, and the data for a particular training session are stored for further use. I transfer the data for a given session to an Excel workbook I developed several years ago. This Excel workbook then generates various graphs; the information that I want is presented so that I see my heart rate (bpm) during most of the rowing sequence and can relate it to my rowing speed (in seconds for 500 meters) and to the rate at which I am rowing (in strokes per minute). The Concept2 data collector also calculates the power output (watts) for each stroke and for entire intervals based on the measured speed.

My Excel workbook takes this information and calculates averages for each rowing interval, for all strokes up to the present stroke in a given stretch, with average cumulative power and average speed. I can plot whatever I want—average heart rate or number of strokes versus time. Sometimes I show all six of these measures in a single plot.

If I look at the power curves for the 500 meter hard segment, I see a rapid decrease in the cumulative curve. At first, I pull as hard as I can (more than 375 watts) for the first few strokes at close to 40 strokes per minute (spm). Then as I decrease my stroke rate to 32 spm or so, my power decreases. The power output stabilizes around 275 watts for the second minute. In other words, I slow down over time because I am no longer capable of pulling with that initial power.

That's life.

Now look at the corresponding heart rate during those nearly two minutes! For this 500 meter hard segment, it rises from 75 to 156 bpm in a beautiful curve, with just a little hiccup during the first few strokes as the stroke rate decreased. Basically, my heart rate control during this major effort looks fantastic. Yours might look the same, if after your midday swim you were to run at top speed from the beach to your house. Just two minutes of top speed running, with panting at the top of the hill.

Now, go to the beginning of the entire rowing session, to those first two warm-up stretches. I row at 20 spm, similar to what I was doing a month earlier when Wout and you walked back after Vince and I had had a bit of a disagreement. Normally, my heart rate might go to 110 bpm during the first and 120 bpm during the second warm-up kilometer. On the graph, I see my heart rate rising from 75 to 125 bpm in a rather noisy pattern and going to 120 to 125 bpm for the first kilometer—it's simply too high. The second kilometer in the diagram is perhaps better. It starts at around 70 bpm, shoots up to 100 bpm, and then proceeds to 120 bpm during the next four minutes. I followed this with a very slow kilometer. However, what I see here is really pathetic heart rate control: down to 85 bpm during the first few strokes, with various bumps up to 115, 130, and settling around 115 bpm.

Basically, what I found was that my system was fine when I needed power and became more chaotic when I was just loafing along during warm-up or resting stretches.

It is as though my heart tells me, "Hey, fella—if we have to work hard, I'll be there to make sure everything is fine. If, however, you are just going to futz around, why should I use my talents to give you a precise and stable heart rate? What's the point?

If you are going to amble to town, I'll pump a bit of blood now and then, but I see no point in doing so in a precise or orderly manner. There is enough blood to go around, and you'll be OK."

It was clear to me that I needed to stabilize my heart rate regulation. Based on my experience of the past seven years, I can do this with nice long workouts preceded by the usual two warm-up and cooldown stretches.

I was greedy however. I wanted to squeeze more performance out of my old carcass, and so I kept doing the 500 meter splits and shorter stuff for the first September week.

I also lowered my daily medication, which has kept me going since 2000, from 100 to 50 mg of flecainide, thinking I had everything under such great control.

Even more stupid, if that can be imagined, I skipped my normal warm-up on the Concept2 in the clubhouse before stepping into the boat. I always start with two 1 km segments for warm-up.

I even left my Polar heart rate monitor and watch in my bag. I'm doing so well . . . why would I need that watch?

Slept badly on September 12.

Had to row at 6:00 a.m. on September 13.

It was unpleasantly cold on the water, and we then went for a single 7-km rather hard stretch. This felt good (or so it seemed).

The combination of all of these ignored precautions, however, was evidently a bit much for my presumed perfect state. When we stopped rowing after the 7 km stretch, after ending with power for the last 500 meters or so, my heart probably thought it had to go down nicely for two minutes to be ready for the next hard interval.

But as we turned around, nothing much happened. The coach had his say and there was some chatter and sipping of drinks as we got ready for the return stretch. Meanwhile, after the first two minutes, my heart rate was probably becoming chaotic, maybe around 120, 130 bpm, whatever. When we started up again, I felt a lack of power; maybe because my heart had nowhere to go in its confused state . . . and from then on, things got worse.

I have been more than lucky.

Hope all is fine with you, Ap.

Veel liefs,

Bernie

· · ·

Things did indeed get worse.

On the day it all happened, he was tired from the bicycle trip in Italy. He had slept poorly the night before.

Then, almost as an "Oh, by the way," he mentions he had reduced his maintenance doses of flecainide down to about one-sixth of the originally recommended dose for VT prevention. On the morning in question, he omitted his warm-up on the Concept2 and left his monitor in the clubhouse.

What was he thinking? Was it pride? Was it just a moment of inattention to detail, sloppiness?

As the crew prepared to head back to the boathouse, Bernie lost consciousness.

Rowing an eight-oared shell with one teammate unconscious poses some really serious problems, but his teammates managed to get him ashore. Without the ICD, his tachycardia degenerated into a full-blown cardiac arrest. The rowing team started CPR and immediately called for help.

With their typical speed and precision, the Swiss paramedics resuscitated Bernie.

CHAPTER 28

Epilogue

After the paramedics defibrillated Bernie and rapidly intubated him on the spot, they took him to the hospital. Once again, he was in intensive care.

For all of his friends and family, the degree of anoxic brain damage associated with his cardiac arrest was the most pressing concern. From Renske's description, he regained consciousness quickly. I didn't see him in the early stages of his recovery.

Bernie and Renske came to visit family and friends in the US about a year after his arrest. We had settled just outside of Ann Arbor, Michigan, and we were delighted to have them stay with us over a weekend. Post–arrest Bernie looked as healthy as the young man who pilfered oranges on our long-ago trip to Florida, and his conversation was as worldly and wide ranging as ever. By the time a year had passed, he had no obvious deficits. His sense of humor, his memory, and his motor skills all appeared intact.

Was there something different? Yes. He seemed like a character from an old Ray Bradbury story who didn't really quite trust his perceptions anymore. After the letter to Appie, he did not add to his journal or pursue his dream of completing a book about his heart. I'm not sure whether the end of his writing was the result of neurological or emotional trauma.

I did not push him on the details of his decisions to reduce his medication doses or row in a sprint race. He was a scientist. He had known Avery's dictum from the start: Happiness is "an experiment that works, *and doing it all the time." He had done the experiment repeatedly and consistently until he changed methods for the Zurich City Sprints. Maybe there was a bit of "I'm going to show you I can do this," a little ego on the line. The smart guys, or the less proud ones, would not have played a game they couldn't win.*

So we stayed on safer conversational ground. My 1963 failure to tape my oarlocks in the President's Cup lost us the race, and Bernie never second-guessed me about that. I wasn't about to second-guess him.

As a couple, Bernie and Renske appeared to have achieved détente on the subject of another ICD. He would not have one implanted, but he had a blue Philips portable ACD, which he always carried with him in a small rucksack.

They had also agreed that he would not row again. I don't know if there were more conversations with his electrophysiology specialists.

As far as I know, he had no more episodes of sustained tachycardia.

• • •

A few months after they returned to Zurich from their visit with us, Bernie called. He had started to experience abdominal pain and major changes in his bowel habits, which he described to me with high good humor and great detail.

Despite extensive testing, his first hospitalization failed to confirm a diagnosis.

Bernie's symptoms worsened. By the time his pancreatic cancer was diagnosed, it had spread widely. Much to my surprise, he opted to undergo chemotherapy. We discussed the chemo regimen in detail, but we did not discuss the reasons for his choice.

After his cardiac arrest, I think Bernie had lost his enthusiasm for living, if not his "will to live." I suspect he wanted some time to spend with Renske and his family and was willing to do whatever was required to gain it. He did, in fact, enjoy a brief remission.

He died on February 28, 2015, survived by his second wife, Renske Heddema; five siblings; Anna (his daughter with his first wife, Margaret Hauschka); and his grandchildren, Skye and Luna.

Postscript

When new research is presented at scientific meetings, an individual expert or sometimes a panel of experts will discuss the findings. The expert's role is to raise important questions about the data, point out pitfalls in the conclusions, and put findings into a broader scientific context.

As a cardiologist looking at Bernie's story, I have three major concerns.

First, what exactly was wrong with Bernie's heart? The documentation of his episodes of VT is overwhelming. But usually, VT is associated with advanced structural and mechanical heart disease.

In his case, the dissociation between the severity of his electrical problems and the relatively well-maintained mechanical function of his heart was striking. There are several possible explanations; two of these possible hypotheses seem most reasonable to me. One is that the primary disease process did not involve the heart itself but was instead a problem involving heart rate control (primarily a neurologic disorder).

Bernie sensed and demonstrated repeatedly that he was vulnerable to arrhythmias in certain situations, which offers some support to this concept, as do the chaotic changes in heart rates noted when he attempted to exercise without the warm-up and cooldown sessions. Additional support comes from the two major episodes of tachycardia that were associated with "irritation" and stress, one at the Zurich Stock Exchange and the other when his older colleague repeatedly interrupted his guest lecture.

Cardiologists have tended to view VT as a random event. As medicine becomes more personalized and more and more data are available from patients with implanted devices, researchers will employ big data techniques to gain more insight into the concept of physiologic, neurologic, and psychological vulnerability.

An alternative hypothesis is that Bernie had a primary cardiomyopathy, with both heart muscle and electrical manifestations. Many patients over the past decade have shown some degree of ejection fraction recovery with widespread use of more effective drugs, such as angiotensin-converting enzyme (ACE) inhibitors and beta-adrenergic blockers. In this scenario, one might postulate that the heart muscle aspect of Bernie's disease responded to the beta-adrenergic blocking treatment (metoprolol succinate) initiated after his ICD, and again to the ACE inhibitors he received after the ICD removal, so that he maintained fairly good pump function.

I don't think we will know until other similar cases come along.

My second concern is that I don't want my telling of Bernie's story to be construed as making a case against implanted cardiac rhythm-control devices. The development of clinically effective pacemakers, implantable defibrillators, and cardiac resynchronization pacing devices stands as one of the great advances of medical technology. The important message that patients and families need to hear about ICDs from Bernie's story is that these devices help manage VT, not cure it. Like everything else physicians can offer, implanting these devices represents a trade-off between benefit and risk

My third and most serious worry is that some readers may interpret this book as an attempt to show Bernie, or his medical behavior, as a role model for other patients. That's absolutely not the case. Far from it! There's no question that many patients with heart disease can benefit from a rehabilitation program that includes controlled exercise, but I certainly would not advocate an unsupervised, strenuous home exercise program like Bernie's for patients with serious arrhythmia. Furthermore, I did not support his repeated unsupervised "tweaking" of medication doses. On top of this, his refusal to get prompt care for his ICD infection was foolhardy, as was turning down another device after the infection was eradicated. On these issues, he was a stubborn Dutchman who damn near killed himself with hubris. To his credit, I think he would smile and agree.

On the other hand, all of us—doctors, patients, and families—can learn from his willingness to carefully think through the questions related to his care and then discuss his questions openly and respectfully with his doctors.

$\cdots$

When I first read Bernie's papers, I wanted to share the message I saw in them. Bernie's clinical course was remarkable. He had some devastating lows (1999, in particular). The low points were offset by his personal triumphs, particularly his team's rowing victories. He sometimes questioned and pushed his physicians. Though he did not always follow their recommendations, he was never hostile or adversarial. He respected them, and they respected him. Most importantly, through the course of his illness, he learned to focus on living his life as fully as possible. As he said, "It will be a lot of work, and that is just how it will always be."

THE BOWMAN

Until very near the end of my writing, I did not realize that this exercise had led me to an extended exploration of the nature of friendship. This story began with two young men's shared experiences: a rigorous curriculum, the amazing science of modern biology, and mutual love of rowing. As we both matured and achieved some degree of professional success, our friendship grew—but it grew because we were tolerant. We were both highly focused and compartmentalized people. Bernie tolerated my introverted, non-communicative nature. I tolerated his opinionated and stubborn nature.

Our long conversation has now come to an end. The bowman always crosses the finish line first.

Top left: Bernard at a lunch in a chateau-hotel/manor where he and Renske celebrated their wedding in 1992. *Top right:* Bernard with his grandchildren, Luna and Skye, while rebuilding their house in Maine in 2010. *Middle left:* Bernard with his daughter Anna at her marriage in Maine in 2006. *Middle center:* Bernard in Maine in 2006. *Middle right:* Bernard in Portugal at the second home of his friends Otto and Susan Wassenaar. *Bottom left:* Bernard and Renske on the rooftop terrace of the University Hospital in July 2014, one week after the final pancreas diagnosis. The ETH and Lake Zurich are in the background. *Bottom right:* Bernard in Maine at Anna's Wedding in 2006.

Part II

FOUR EASY
PIECES

These essays show Bernie's teaching at its best. They are included to give readers a sense of what he was like in the classroom.

Macromolecules:
A Little Biology

In this essay, Bernie describes a conceptual world. In the laboratory, we can only "see" small molecules and chemical bonds indirectly, with sophisticated instruments. Yet, when he describes this world inside the cell, the structures of the molecules are as real to him as everyday objects.

And, once again, Bernie editorializes against the potato, shares his thoughts on how we know old friends, and uses his cereal box to show that the process of evolution involves losses as well as gains.

• • •

Macromolecules (very large molecules) consist of smaller molecules. In some cases, such as for polysaccharides, identical small molecules are simply linked together to form long chains. Starch is such a macromolecule, a long chain of many glucose molecules. These chains are not always linear. Branches can occur, so that after every 50 or 100 glucose molecules in a chain, another long glucose chain branches off, while the original chain extends farther. If there are many branches, the resulting macromolecule looks something like a tree with many or fewer branches, each again having branches. If a cell were to need a long rope for some reason, it would make sense to wind several long linear starch macromolecules around one another, creating a long molecular rope. If the cell were to require a thicker and shorter piece of material for some purpose, it might prefer to have branched starch molecules clumping together. So, the cell can use a molecule as seemingly simple as glucose, also called dextrose, which some of us carry around as a supply of instant energy, to make various structures for a variety of purposes.

Now when we eat a potato, we eat starch of both varieties: long linear chains and branched chains. The same is true for rice, corn, wheat, and other cereals. The difference is that rice and wheat are dry, with very little water. Corn contains more water, and potatoes consist of 80% water, 18.5% starch, and 1.5% protein. If you go hiking for a week and have to make a choice between potatoes and rice as your staple, rice is the much better option unless you plan to hike in very arid areas with few, if any, water sources. Here potatoes are probably better than a combination of rice and extra water carried in a canister that adds weight to your backpack. Rice has one major plus compared to potatoes; it contains 12-18% protein in addition to 80% starch, with just a few percent water. So, those who eat rice rather than potatoes require less additional protein, obtained from meat, fish, or other protein-rich vegetables. Hence the Brazilian *feijoada*, a combination of inexpensive rice, beans, and cornmeal, which is a fairly complete dish, even without meat.

· · ·

DNA is a long chain that consists of four different molecules: adenine, guanine, cytosine, and thymine, abbreviated as A, G, C, T.

The nucleic acid monomers are compounds called purines and pyrimidines, each linked to a small sugar molecule. DNA monomers differ a little from the RNA monomers, but that is not relevant for this discussion. The important point here is not only that the biopolymers DNA and RNA contain 4 different monomers but that these are *no longer distributed randomly* along the length of the chains formed with these monomers.

The number of theoretically possible variants is 1^{100}. If we do the calculation including the 16 possible doublets per two bases in the DNA or RNA, the number of variants increases to about 1^{120}, or a 1 followed by 120 zeroes. One single cell of ours contains chromosomes with a total of about 3 billion bases in the DNA, equivalent to about 15 million of the 200 base pieces discussed above. If we were to try to store all of the 1^{120} possible 200 base pieces, we would pack the entire known universe, and there would still be a lot of DNA left over. All of this applies only to the variations possible in a piece of DNA with 200 bases. In fact, a typical gene contains around 1,000 bases. The number of possible variants is unlimited.

Despite this, each of us contains a set of very specific genes, and the differences from one person to any other person on Earth are no more than 1% of the entire DNA sequences present in our cells.

We vary in a specific manner, thanks to the fantastic specificity of our DNA-synthesizing machinery. This machinery reliably copies the DNA that we received from our parents in almost equal measure, with their traits mixed and recombined to make us similar to, yet different from, both of them. And, as we age, this machinery maintains our original DNA information such that your friends who last saw you ten years ago still recognize you, your charms and your peculiarities, today.

• • •

Proteins are biopolymers, too. Proteins, however, consist of different groups of monomers, and they are polymerized in different ways. Instead of a DNA or RNA chain that is built with a sugar backbone from which the purines or pyrimidines protrude, proteins are polymers built from amino acids that are linked together by peptide bonds.

As is the case for DNA and RNA, the amino-acid monomers that are linked to build a protein follow a specific pattern.

All of the monomers that occur in proteins are "amino-acids," so-called because they are organic acids with carbon, hydrogen, and at least one oxygen atom and all containing one or more nitrogen atoms. A few amino acids also contain a sulfur atom. There are 20 different amino acids that make up the monomer set that constitutes proteins. These small amino-acid molecules vary widely in their structure and properties; their variability means that proteins also have differing properties that depend both on the amino acids from which they are made and on the sequence in which the amino acids are linked together.

The range of different possible proteins is endless. This becomes easier to imagine when we consider the hundreds of amino acids in a particular protein and the fact that at every position in the sequence, almost any one of 20 amino acids can occur. (In practice, there are some limitations on which amino acids fit in a particular position. The ease with which an amino acid fits between its neighbors depends on who those neighbors happen to be. This hardly affects the endless number of possible sequences.)

Sometimes proteins are assembled into larger machines that produce more complex structures. Since some are tools and others have structural functions, there may be many copies of a particular protein in a single cell. In addition to biocatalytic roles, helping build and break down small molecules, some proteins have roles in regulatory systems, receiving and sensing an input from some source in the cell or in the external environment around the cell or transmitting a signal to actuate a mechanism that operates somewhere within the cell.

Consider the humble bacterium, so small that we can pack one trillion of them on the tip of our pinky. It must produce all of these macromolecules; coordinate the amounts of all of them; make sure that it makes all of the amino acids, vitamins, sugars, bases, and so on needed to reproduce itself by first growing to double its length; then divide without the two halves falling apart; and finally end up with two identical bacteria. It does all this in a few hours, alone in nature, with a little sugar and some salts. It can carry off this same marvelous reproduction in 30 minutes in the lab, if we feed it properly, so it doesn't have to do all the work alone.

If you take a look at your breakfast cereal box, you will see we get at least 10 of the amino acids and a variety of vitamins, in addition to wheat, corn, or rice, from those prepared cereals. The cereal box is telling you that we cannot do what these bacteria, each by itself, can do. We do a lot, and we are more complex. We consist of larger cells that interact to produce more sophisticated beings, but along the way we have lost some of the synthetic abilities available to most organisms a billion years ago.

• • •

Bernie and I belonged to a generation of students for whom the structure and function of DNA was new and exciting information. Watson and

*Crick published their double-helix model for DNA just a decade before
we were introduced to it in college.*[32]

*Students today encounter basic genetics as a fully established branch
of science. In contrast, Bernie had watched the science develop, and for him,
the excitement never faded. You can hear it here, as he plays his shell game
of rapidly increasing numbers, followed by "Quite obviously, the number
of possible variants is unlimited" and the Witholt smile.*

*The charm of Bernie's intellect was his ability to connect his science
to the everyday world, with his steadfast aversion to packing potatoes on
hikes and his absolute delight "that your friends who last saw you ten
years ago still recognize you, your charms and your peculiarities, today."*

---

32 Watson, J. D. and Crick, F. H. C. "A structure for deoxyribose nucleic acid." Nature
171: 737–738 (1953).

Cell Membranes

This essay is Bernie at play with numbers, just for the fun of figuring out that a liter of lipid membrane material could cover about 40 acres. This is what scientists do.

He delighted in using exponents and manipulating large numbers. He talked continuously and went through the math so fast that anyone watching soon felt pretty sure there was a con in it someplace. But where?

• • •

Membranes surround each of our cells. In addition, cells also contain internal membranes that define the various structures within the cell with wonderful names that have been used to denote what microscopists have seen as their tools improved over the years: the nucleus that contains our DNA, and the lysosomes, the endoplasmic reticulum, and the Golgi complex.

To get an idea of how much membrane material there is in our tissues, we can begin by determining the amount of lipid material present in our bodies. Some of us have more than average amounts of lipids and fats in our bodies, but typically about 5–10% of our dry mass consists of lipids that form the membranes around and within our cells. So, an average 70 kg person, who is only about 30% solid mass, consists of about 21 kg of solids of which 1 to 2 kg are lipids.

How large a surface can these lipids cover? Lipids have a density of about 1.0 g per milliliter, which is identical to that of water. So, one kg of lipids will have a volume of one liter or a little more than a quart. This quart contains 100% lipids (or fats). So, here we are with this liter of pure lipid. If we spread it out, it will cover a very large surface. The size of this surface will increase as we spread the lipids more thinly. The thickness of a lipid bilayer is about 4–6 nanometers, which is about how thinly they are spread in our bodies, around and inside each and every cell. There are exceptions, as usual, but let's consider these single layers for now.

Okay. If we spread this material out until it has a uniform thickness (thinness) of 5 nanometers, we'll end up with a total surface area of 1 with 24 zeroes, divided by 5, which is a 2 with 23 zeroes, or 2×10^{23} square nanometers (nm^2). So, our 2×10^{23} nm^2 equals 2×10^5 square meters and, since a single hectare is 10,000 m^2, one liter of lipid material can produce a membrane surface of $1.5–2^{23}$ $nm^2 = 1.5–2^5 m^2 = 15–20$ hectare, or 35 to 45 acres.

These types of "calculations" do not produce precise numbers. However, they are not "guesstimates." We make these types of estimates to give us an idea of the scale, relative sizes, amounts of material, total areas, and volumes involved in these complicated biological structures.

• • •

Have a careful look at The Conjurer, *painted by another crafty Dutchman, Hieronymus Bosch.*[33]

---

33   http://boschproject.org/#/artworks/The_Conjurer_Musee_Municipal

On Cells and Their Membranes

All cells are bounded by a membrane that separates the internal space from the external space. This membrane is far more than a passive bag around the cell. It is, in fact, a very complex structure that not only retains the contents of the cell but also allows different molecules to be transported into or secreted out of the cell. This gets complicated; for example, the cell membrane must allow glucose to enter without allowing molecules that are smaller or similar in other ways to exit.

Various pumps and channels that bring specifically desired molecules in and pump undesired (waste or foreign) molecules out cover the boundary cell membrane. These pumps typically consist of one or more highly specialized protein molecules, and producing, running, and maintaining all these pumps costs the cell energy and effort. To minimize this effort, the cell possesses mechanisms to sense which molecules are nearby in its neighborhood and suitable for transportation inward. Based on the sensed information, the cell may then turn on the protein synthesis machinery to make the desired pumps, if it has this information available. Those cells that do are more likely to survive than those that do not. After a few generations, only those that can transport useful chemicals into their little "bodies" will have survived. In other words, we see natural selection at work in the evolution of bacterial populations.

Single-celled organisms such as bacteria, yeasts, and fungi are directly exposed to their environment, however wild this might be. They are protected by a harder cell wall formed just outside the cell membrane, much as plant cells are. A tree can stand tall because its individual cells have walls with sufficient strength to keep the cell from being compressed like a little balloon. Trees with their thicker cell walls form woods that are harder, stronger, and heavier than other plants with weaker cell walls.

Cell walls are stiff and hard, while the underlying cell membranes must be flexible and impermeable, with sophisticated pumps to enable the transit of specific molecules. All of this must be combined with the ability to adapt and expand as cells grow and divide. Membranes must be capable of expanding, of accommodating many different protein pumps, and of spatially organizing the cellular tools that have assembly line-like properties.

This is where fats and lipids come in. These interesting molecules have two functional parts. One part likes water; the other likes oil. Lipids will form little spheres, with the oily tails inside and the polar heads facing out, on the surface of the spheres. As more lipids are added to the sphere, a sheet forms with two sets of lipids, the oil-loving non-polar tails facing inwards and water-loving polar heads on the outer surfaces. We refer to these sheets as "bilayers": the two layers of lipid. In a cell, these bilayers arrange themselves with their oily, non-polar parts aligned, leaving the polar or water-loving portion of each molecule to face the watery or aqueous environment both inside and outside the cell. So, a lipid-containing cell will almost spontaneously form a membrane between the inner cell space and the outer watery environment, whether that cell is in a river, a drop of water on a leaf, a liquid in a laboratory, or a large beer fermenter at your local brewery.

* * *

At a practical level, Novocain and many other anesthetics are "non-polar" molecules that get caught up within the membranes of our nerve cells. The anesthetic alters the function of the nerve cell membrane so that it does not transmit the pain sensations that we would otherwise feel in the dentist's chair.

* * *

Think about this short essay the next time you visit the dentist. While she drills, you will be both pain-free and happy that you know about bilayers.

In the last half of the twentieth century, pharmacology evolved rapidly from a collection of empirical knowledge about "materia medica" to a rigorous scientific discipline based on cell physiology, biochemistry, and computer modeling. Bernie was fascinated by the cellular mechanisms of drug effects.

ESSAY 4

Bioinformatics

The access to information that the Internet provides delighted Bernie personally. However, as a teacher and researcher, he also saw the very real danger of ideas that were not supported by solid experimental data. In this final essay, he closes with a carefully phrased warning.

• • •

In the 21st century, we have online libraries, mountains of information on the web. But one still must read, evaluate, judge, think, correlate, and most of all, write. Clicking is not enough.

Before any of that, we must have a direction. We have to formulate questions, and they must be specific, precise questions. That takes practice. That is why four years of research on the way to a PhD is good training for whatever comes afterwards.

Fifty years ago, we used research libraries. Everything worth recording (and a lot that wasn't) was written up in papers that were then published in scientific journals. Eugene Garfield described this process in the late 1950s and early 60s while he was developing easier ways to wade through all these papers on the way to new insights. He wrote that there were approximately 100,000 different journals worldwide that covered topics from gardening to particle physics. No library could afford to subscribe to all of these journals. (The number 100,000 may have been apocryphal.) Garfield went on to say that 173 journals covered 80% of material that was, at some point, cited in subsequent work either by the original authors or others.

For any given field, for example English poetry, economics, physical chemistry, genetics, or anatomy, 6 to 12 carefully chosen journals would suffice to cover most of the developments in the field. Many academic libraries subscribed to substantially more journals, but even less well-endowed schools were able to afford a basic set of 200 to 500 journals.

Still, finding papers of interest meant looking at the monthly, bimonthly, or sometimes half-yearly issues of at least a dozen journals. Garfield began to work with a new weekly journal, *Current Contents*, which listed the index page of each of the journals in a particular major area: physics, chemistry, life sciences, medical sciences, social sciences and so on. One could now scan these indices and decide which papers should be looked at or perhaps collected.

Garfield developed another quite useful tool. Instead of going back in time, looking at references used in a given paper, which tells us how the present paper came to be, Garfield went forward in time and listed how often a given paper was cited, as well as when, where, and by whom. For any paper we can see two trees. One goes backward and tells us the many earlier works that were involved in developing the particular paper of interest. The second tree, going forward in time, tells us the later work that was based, in part, on the particular paper of interest. Both trees are wonderfully useful. We can look backwards and see how a given idea, a notion, a result has developed. We can also look forward and see how it continues to develop, what new and sometimes unexpected insights it led or is leading to.

Back in the mid-60s, we had to go to the library to look at the new information that was added to Garfield's Citation Index each quarter. Today, using my computer, I can access all this information within seconds, once I decide what I want. Every university and good-size company is permanently linked to these systems. As long as I am associated with a university, a company, or even the entire university system of a country, for instance good old Brazil (which actually does have national contracts with the providers of all this citation and other research information), I can see and download any and all of this information.

I have access to the finest mental ice cream forever and in unlimited amounts.

• • •

In the life sciences, we have an important bioinformatics discipline. Large pharma and chemical companies clamor for talent in this area. More and more early work is done with computer programs using so-called "*in silico*" approaches. Often this complements what we do in the laboratory, "*in vitro*," harkening back to the distant past of glass beakers and flasks.

When we undertake these *in silico* flights of imagination, we must tie them to reality at the start and at the end. These connections become especially important before we launch the next flight. If we accept too many loose ends, then we cannot distinguish our dreams and hopes from reality.

About the Author

Bernard in 2003 in the North Sea near Leiden, where his first grand-child, Skye, had just been born.

BERNARD WITHOLT was born in Holland shortly after the Nazi invasion in 1941. After the end of World War II, the family moved to Brazil, living in both São Paulo and Rio de Janeiro. In 1959, they immigrated to the United States and settled in Pennsylvania.

With the support of his high school guidance counselor, Bernard gained a full scholarship to Amherst College. He graduated in 1964 and then took his PhD at Johns Hopkins University, which was followed by post–doctoral work at the University of California, San Diego.

He spent his professional life in Europe, first as a faculty member at the University of Groningen in the Netherlands and then, from 1992 until his retirement, at ETH Zurich, a world-class research university with ties to more than twenty Nobel prizewinners.

His research groups did foundational work in microbial biotechnology, and he was widely recognized by his peers as among the most original, provocative, and productive people in the field—as a teacher and mentor as well as an innovator.

In 2007, the Dutch royal family recognized Bernard's work with its highest civilian honor, The Order of The Netherlands Lion (De Orde van de Nederlandse Leeuw). The award is given for exceptional achievements in art, science, and literature. He was cited primarily for his work in Groningen, where, in addition to his research and teaching, he founded a science park and several start-up ventures.

About the Editor

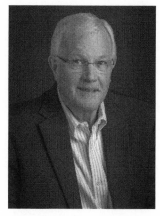

ROGER MILLS graduated from Amherst College and the University of Pennsylvania School of Medicine. After his medical internship and residency at the Hospital of the University of Pennsylvania and two years active duty in the US Navy, he completed his training in cardiology at Harvard's Peter Bent Brigham Hospital. His thirty-year clinical career included medical directorship of the heart transplant program at the University of Florida, where he was a professor of medicine, and a subsequent appointment as a staff cardiologist at the Cleveland Clinic.

In 2005, he joined Janssen Pharmaceuticals, and over the next ten years held various positions, including vice president for medical affairs at Scios Inc. and senior director at Janssen Research & Development, LLC.

Dr. Mills is a fellow of the American College of Physicians and the American College of Cardiology and a senior fellow of the Society for Cardiac Angiography and Interventions. He has served on the editorial boards of the *Journal of the American College of Cardiology*, the *American Journal of Cardiology*, and *Clinical*

Cardiology. In 2009, he received the Simon Dack Award for Out-standing Scholarship from the American College of Cardiology.

In addition to extensive research publications, Roger is the author of *Nesiritide: The Rise and Fall of Scios,* the Foreword Indies 2016 Bronze Medal winner for science. He writes a personal blog, theweeklypacket.com, and maintains a website, rmillsmd.com.